"Church history can be daunting, es[...] y
teachers. Yet it has played a massiv[...])
better than Jennifer Woodruff Tait, [...] 1
the subject (*Christian History*), a part-time minister, and fantastic teacher, to get
us over our fears and introduce us to some of the most important episodes in the
Christian tradition. This is a clear, fair-minded, and reliable introduction to the
most important subject you have yet to understand. Warmly recommended."

Douglas A. Sweeney, dean and professor of divinity at Beeson Divinity School, Samford University

"Jennifer Woodruff Tait thinks that study of the Christian past provides 'navigation
charts' to help believers sail safely through the turbulent waters of the present. Her
sharply focused attention to seven key sentences from strategic moments in the
history of Christianity demonstrates the wisdom of her metaphor. This book is an
ideal resource (with another metaphor) to begin mining the riches of the past for
the best kind of wisdom in the present."

Mark Noll, author of *Turning Points: Strategic Moments in the History of Christianity*

"Jennifer Woodruff Tait tells the story of Christianity with energy, clarity, and au-
dacity. There is no musty smell of the past here. The epoch-making conflicts and
the breathtaking creativity described in this book are still with us. Succinct and
engaging, this introduction gives readers an appreciation for some of the biggest
moments in church history."

Daryl R. Ireland, research assistant professor of world Christianity and associate director of the
Center for Global Christianity and Mission, Boston University

"This book is just what the author says it is: a clear and helpful map to a historical
terrain that deserves much more exploration today than it usually gets—especially
from Christians, who have the most reason to explore it. What makes it such a
helpful book is that it is written in exactly the style that such a book needs.
C. S. Lewis once claimed to have been, in essence, a 'medieval man,' who thought
and wrote in many ways through the sensibilities of that era. Since I first read her
writing, I've thought that Jennifer Woodruff Tait writes with the clarity and force
of the eighteenth-century *philosophes* (and even better, with the orthodox faith that
eluded most of those penetrating French thinkers). In fact, that clarity and force
and faith she shares with Lewis, whom we both admire. To my mind these traits of
Dr. Tait's writing, along with the synoptic vantage point she has gained from her
long and wise service as editor of the beloved *Christian History* magazine, guar-
antee that this book will prove the perfect navigation aid for this generation of
students—and for readers of all ages—in their historical explorations."

Chris R. Armstrong, author of *Medieval Wisdom for Modern Christians*, program fellow, Kern
Family Foundation (Wisconsin)

"This book is full of sensible and occasionally surprising decisions, all of them elegantly expressed. It has something for everyone—theological disputation, political intrigue, spiritual insight, and a touch of drama. Tait has managed the seemingly impossible task of distilling the church's history into a slender volume. Best of all, she imbues that history with a sense of tradition. One feels the gravity and freedom that comes with taking up the Christian tradition as one's own. This is church history as it should be, written for any and for all."

Justus H. Hunter, assistant professor of church history at United Theological Seminary

"Jennifer Woodruff Tait has given us a real gift in *Christian History in Seven Sentences*. This slim volume is stuffed with substance. Along with the major narratives, it includes an amazing number of brief references that connect people, movements, and ideas, and prompt further reading. The book seamlessly weaves theological explanation and historical background, reinforcing the conviction that God's actions and human agency interact mysteriously and truly for God's great saving purposes. And it's all done through sparkling prose. Lay readers will find this book a helpful introduction to Christian history, and pastors needing a refresher, a joyful goad. This is the kind of work needed to help people grow deeply in the faith."

Steve Rankin, director, Spiritual Maturity Project

"Jennifer Woodruff Tait has expertly succeeded at the monumental task of summing up the history of Christianity in just seven formative sentences. Tait's approach is accessible, readable, and engaging. Readers will gain a clear sense of the scope and trajectory of Christianity's intricate story in broad strokes from the church's birth at Pentecost to the Edinburgh Conference and Vatican II of the twentieth century. In the end, the reader should be left without any doubt that our engagement with the Christians of the past is crucial to our lives as Christians in the present."

Jennifer Powell McNutt, Dyrness Associate Professor of Biblical and Theological Studies, Wheaton College

"Four features of this superb book stand out: First, the writing. It is consistently lucid yet thought-filled, witty yet serious. Second, the erudition. The notes and bibliographic essay alone are worth the price of admission. Third, the conciseness. Jennifer Woodruff Tait brings the entire sweep of (mostly) Western Christian history into view through the deft device of isolating, exegeting, and contextualizing key sentences in the tradition's story. Finally, the import. Foregrounding not only her own Christian faith but also the implications of such faith for the church today, Tait answers the 'So what?' question clearly, decisively, and with a pastor's heart."

Grant Wacker, Gilbert T. Rowe Distinguished Professor Emeritus of Christian History, Duke Divinity School

CHRISTIAN HISTORY

IN SEVEN SENTENCES

A SMALL INTRODUCTION TO A VAST TOPIC

JENNIFER WOODRUFF TAIT

Academic

An imprint of InterVarsity Press
Downers Grove, Illinois

InterVarsity Press
P.O. Box 1400, Downers Grove, IL 60515-1426
ivpress.com
email@ivpress.com

InterVarsity Press® is the book-publishing division of InterVarsity Christian Fellowship/USA®, a movement of students and faculty active on campus at hundreds of universities, colleges, and schools of nursing in the United States of America, and a member movement of the International Fellowship of Evangelical Students. For information about local and regional activities, visit intervarsity.org.

Scripture quotations, unless otherwise noted, are from the New Revised Standard Version Bible, copyright © 1989 National Council of the Churches of Christ in the United States of America. Used by permission. All rights reserved worldwide.

The publisher cannot verify the accuracy or functionality of website URLs used in this book beyond the date of publication.

Cover design: David Fassett
Interior design: Beth McGill
Image: Vintage paper © tomograf / iStock / Getty Images Plus

ISBN 978-0-8308-5477-6 (print)
ISBN 978-0-8308-5478-3 (digital)

Printed in the United States of America ♾

InterVarsity Press is committed to ecological stewardship and to the conservation of natural resources in all our operations. This book was printed using sustainably sourced paper.

Library of Congress Cataloging-in-Publication Data
A catalog record for this book is available from the Library of Congress.

P	25	24	23	22	21	20	19	18	17	16	15	14	13	12	11	10	9	8	7	6	5	4	3	2	1
Y	38	37	36	35	34	33	32	31	30	29	28	27	26	25	24	23	22	21

For my father

John Hurlbut Woodruff

February 6, 1935–January 18, 2019

Hold to Christ, and for the rest be uncommitted.

HERBERT BUTTERFIELD

CONTENTS

ACKNOWLEDGMENTS

About ten years ago, I wrote a book. It was a great experience, but I didn't foresee my life ever moving in that direction again. However, when the opportunity arose to contribute to this series, I couldn't resist; I've always seen my primary mission as making history accessible to the person on the street. But I never would have gotten here without significant assistance.

First of all, I want to thank my colleagues at *Christian History* magazine for the collegial working atmosphere that has gotten me through the editing of thirty-four issues (as of this writing). Overseeing a magazine that covers all eras, movements, and people in church history has given me a broad and deep background from which to tell this story. Plus, these fine people gave me time off to help me finish! Thank you so much to Bill Curtis, Chris Armstrong, Dawn Moore, Kaylena Radcliff, Dan Graves, Meg Moss, Doug Johnson, and Max Pointner.

I also want to thank Grant Wacker for, long ago, believing in me as a doctoral student. Without him there would have been no first book, and hence no second one. I owe you a thousand sarsaparillas, Grant.

Then, I am grateful to David McNutt, my editor at InterVarsity Press, for suggesting the idea, believing it could be done, and waiting patiently and graciously for me to do it.

It has been my great pleasure to serve two churches as a part-time priest during the writing of this book and to participate in the worship life of several others. The debates and the affirmations of church history ultimately work themselves out in the worship and service of local congregations. At Saint Mark's Episcopal Church (Hazard, KY), Saint John's Episcopal Church (Corbin, KY), the Episcopal Church of Our Saviour (Richmond, KY), and First United Methodist Church (Richmond, KY), there are people who love the Lord, believe the gospel, and serve the world, and I would not have made it this far without them.

I wrote quite a lot of this book at a holiday cottage near Madley in Herefordshire, England. Simon Lockett and the Wye Dore Parishes welcomed my family into the life of the parish for a week—and I got to see a two-thousand-year-old yew tree. If you visit, go to the Hub and get some homebakes, and come back on Sunday for Eucharist. Having coffee in the nave of a church founded in the sixth century will change you.

Finally, what I owe my family is incalculable. I always know I can depend on my brother and sister-in-law Jonathan and Melissa Woodruff and nephew Will for general love and support—and on my in-laws, R. Barry and Trudy Harvey Tait, for probing questions, faithful Christian witness, proofreading, and lunch. The sharp intellects and passion for a just world of my daughters, Catherine Elanor and Elizabeth Beatrice, teach me the meaning of Proverbs 27:17 every single day.

My husband, Edwin, knows the answer to everything I've ever asked him (and answers more quickly than Google); is a full partner in parenting and homemaking; loaned me a few unpublished conceptual paragraphs on purgatory for chapter five; and loves all things that are good and true and beautiful. Indeed, a star shone on the hour of our meeting.

Just before my first book came out, my mother, Marilyn Delle Stanger Woodruff, died. Just before this one came out, my father, John Hurlbut Woodruff, died. Above all I thank them, and offer in their memory the famed prayer from the Cambridge Lessons and Carols service: "Lastly, let us remember before God all those who rejoice with us, but upon another shore, and in a greater light, that multitude which no man can number, whose hope was in the Word made flesh, and with whom in the Lord Jesus we are forever one."

Mom got the first book. Dad gets this one.

INTRODUCTION

Don't know much about history . . ." Sam Cooke sang those lyrics in 1960, but they're just as relevant today. From high schools to graduate schools, in person-on-the-street interviews and conversations with the rich and famous, in attempts to start business and to govern countries, the current tide is turning away from the study of history. As a society, we seek out the new, the entrepreneurial, the scientific. As individuals, we hold the stereotype that we just need to memorize a bunch of names and dates in order to understand the past. As Christians, what should our response be?

For a long time, some branches of Christianity have been fearful of too much study of history as well—especially of the first fifteen hundred years or so of the church's growth and development. We place them in the category of "tradition," sometimes of "unbiblical tradition," and focus on learning other aspects of the Christian life. We want to know what the Bible teaches us is good to do and what we should do today.

But our faith is a historical faith. Its truth rests on claims about history. We claim that an obscure Jewish rabbi really existed in the first century, born of a virgin peasant Galilean girl; that this rabbi taught his disciples certain things about God, life, and moral behavior; that he proclaimed himself to be the fulfillment of millennia of past events in the life of the Hebrew people; that he was executed as a common criminal when he was in his early thirties; and that, in contrast to everyone else who has ever been executed in the history of the human race, he rose from the dead, started a movement, and ascended into heaven promising to send his Spirit to guide the fledgling movement and to come back some day.

We readily admit that all of those are *theological* claims. But it is also true that they are *historical* claims. In fact, the traditional labels BC ("before Christ") and AD (*anno Domini,* "year of our Lord") for the years before and after Bethlehem make the bold historical claim that this is the event to end all other events; this is the hinge on which history turns, the moment at which history changed. And as we begin to explore what happened after Jesus Christ ascended into heaven and the Holy Spirit descended on the disciples, we begin to bridge the gap that exists between what the Bible teaches us to do and what we should do today.

As we try to understand how Jesus' first followers coped with everything that had happened to them and what they did next, we are led very quickly from the study of the Bible into the history of the Christian church. Over twenty centuries, believers have looked to the reports of what Jesus and his followers said and did—our New Testament—and the account of previous generations of his people, the Hebrews—our Old Testament—and decided that it meant certain things for their belief and behavior. Sometimes, we think in hindsight, they got some things wrong. Sometimes we think they seem to have gotten it exactly right. But to cast out onto the waters of Christian living while ignoring the navigation charts these believers have laid out for us would be a dangerous enterprise. They can tell us where the rocks and shoals and waterfalls and sandbars are, and also where there is clear sailing.

This brief book is an attempt to help you put together that navigation chart. It focuses on seven sentences from important documents in church history and uses each sentence to explain the events and people that produced it and resulted from it. There *are* names, and there *are* dates in this book, but the focus is on the narrative—how the story of Christ's followers developed from those earliest days after Pentecost to today. At the end of each chapter, there are recommendations of books that will help you learn more about that specific time and place, and I encourage you to pursue them, but my promise to you is that at the end of *this* book you will have the outline of the whole map.

Surveying the Seven

We begin right where the New Testament leaves off—with Jesus' followers after Pentecost. Our first chapter explores how the early church went from being a persecuted religious minority to the religion of the empire in only three centuries. It spends some time with the Emperor Constantine and how his decision to tolerate Christianity changed the trajectory of the church—first expressed in the Edict of Milan (313), from which this chapter's sentence is drawn: "No one whatsoever should be denied the opportunity to give his heart to the observance of the Christian religion." As we look at the story of the first three hundred years of Christianity, we'll think about the relationship of Christianity to empire today and what lessons about that relationship we can learn from the early church.

For our second sentence, we stay mostly in the fourth century with the Nicene Creed (set forth in 325, altered in 381, and confirmed in 451): "Light from Light, true God from true God, begotten not made, of one substance with the Father." From the perspective of the twenty-first century, we may ask, Why are we spending so much time in the early church? Understanding how rulers and church leaders and theologians figured out what Jesus' life, death, and resurrection meant is crucial to our discipleship. We worship a trinitarian God, and we have a Savior who is both fully human and fully divine, and those things have huge implications for how he saves us and how we follow him. But how did the church come to formulate those doctrines? This chapter explains how the Council of Nicaea tried to settle these issues— and how other councils followed, establishing the calling of councils as a way for the church to move forward practically and theologically. It also explains the growing wealth, power, and political involvement of the church.

We begin to think about one form of protest against that growing wealth and power with our third sentence from *The Rule of Saint Benedict* (c. 530): "And so we are going to establish a school for the service of the Lord." This chapter explains the early development of monasticism as a way to counteract the church's this-worldly power. Benedict's attempt wasn't the first to set out a rule of rigorous discipleship, but in the West it became the most famous and significant. We'll look at the content of *The Rule,* and how Benedict's desire to gather a community around him and give his monks a guide for living changed the complexion of Western Christianity over the next thousand years and left marks on our own practice of spiritual disciplines today.

The very introduction of the term *Western* Christianity, though, leads us to think about how the form of the faith in the West came to be separate from the Eastern form. Our fourth sentence, from the excommunication of Patriarch Kerularios in the East by Pope Leo IX and his legate Cardinal Humbert in the West in 1054 states: "We have sensed here both a great good, whence we greatly rejoice in the Lord, and the greatest evil, whence we lament in misery." The Eastern and Western branches of Christianity grew apart in both practical and theological

matters during the early Middle Ages, until in 1054 they mutually excommunicated each other. Continued negotiations between popes and Byzantine emperors afterward could not stem
the deteriorating relationship, and the Crusades sealed the deal,
with the tragic recognition that the East and West had become
two separate churches.

But this was not the end of schism and separation within the
one body of Christ. With our fifth sentence, we visit the sixteenth
century and Martin Luther's *Ninety-Five Theses* (1517): "When our
Lord and Master Jesus Christ said, 'Repent,' he willed the entire
life of believers to be one of repentance." Luther's insights into the
relationship of law and grace arrived at a time when many recognized the Western church was in need of reform. Indeed, although his work was by no means the first or the only effort to
reform the church, what happened with Luther and his contem-
poraries has been called by many historians not just a reform but
the Reformation. We'll learn about the personal and historical
events that led Luther to compose the *Theses* and the immediate
and long-term results as western Europe was split into a number
of competing Protestant confessions—some deriving directly
from Luther's work, others from similar reform movements that
arose around the same time. And we'll look at how Catholicism
regrouped in response, including by calling the Council of
Trent—a council whose importance is perhaps equal only to
Nicaea and to the council that produced our final sentence.

Before we get there, though, we need to understand what historians call the "modern" era, roughly stretching from the end
of the Reformation to the present day. Christians have always
been involved in mission, but we'll look at the beginnings of a
concerted effort to preach the gospel to the ends of the world as
new developments in technology and transportation made that
possible. By doing so, we'll arrive at our sixth sentence, from the

Edinburgh Conference of 1910: "The church is confronted today, as in no preceding generation, with a literally worldwide opportunity to make Christ known." One of the most significant conferences ever called by Protestant Christians, Edinburgh profoundly influenced Christian mission and ecumenical cooperation and led people to hope for—in the words of John Mott, presider at Edinburgh and founder of the World Council of Churches—"the evangelization of the world in this generation."

As Christians wrestled with all the problems raised by the modern world for belief and mission, Catholics called a council of their own, the Second Vatican Council (1962–1965). From one of its documents, *Gaudium et Spes,* we take our last sentence: "Hence this Second Vatican Council, having probed more profoundly into the mystery of the Church, now addresses itself without hesitation, not only to the sons of the Church and to all who invoke the name of Christ, but to the whole of humanity." Indeed, the effects of Vatican II were not limited to Roman Catholicism. The council resulted in an unforeseen transformation of Catholic worship and relations with other Christians, and this led to far-reaching changes in the worship and outreach of many Protestant groups and attempts to reach ecumenical consensus on some issues debated as far back as the fourth century.

UNDERSTANDING OUR BROTHERS AND SISTERS

By the time we've drawn the whole map and you have it in hand, there are several things I hope you will have learned. The first is that studying history in a Christian context is a conversation—a conversation between us and our brothers and sisters in Christ who lived in the past.[1] And it is a conversation we need to enter into with an expectation of charity, just as in conversations with the brothers and sisters in Christ in our churches today. We may not always agree with everything our predecessors in the faith said or did, but we need to try to understand why they said and did it. They can teach us many good things about the gospel that we might otherwise have forgotten; and sometimes we can come to the conclusion that at a particular moment in time their actions were not in harmony with the gospel, and that we can do better.

The second thing I hope you will learn is that we can always add to our map. Inevitably, any history of the church—especially a brief introduction like this—will have to make choices and will leave something out. As this book is being written primarily for Western readers, we will "zoom in" from time to time on issues of particular interest to Western Christianity. But I hope to at least fill in the outlines of the whole globe so that you have a sense of the size of the map and so that you know where to go exploring when you head off in that direction.

That leads me to my final point. When we look at our road map, we can see that early Christians sought to be in unity as they followed Christ—a unity described in the fourth-century creed that we'll address in chapter two as "one, holy, catholic and apostolic." We can also see that these four adjectives don't really describe the Christian scene as we witness it in the twenty-first century. We will learn, as we travel along our map, that the church has wrestled with issues of unity, doctrine, and faithfulness from its beginnings. As we pursue the decisions and scriptural interpretations that led us from the book of Acts to today's global movement, let us also pray that we grow closer to what Jesus prayed in John 15:12: "This is my commandment, that you love one another as I have loved you."

one

THE EDICT OF MILAN (313)

"No one whatsoever should be denied the opportunity to give his heart to the observance of the Christian religion."

With these words, two Roman emperors changed the course of Christianity forever.[1] The church we read about in the New Testament—and may well have heard about in childhood stories of heroic Christians standing against pagan persecutors—was an illegal faith. Scholars in recent years have debated how often and when it was most persecuted. However, though some of its adherents did increase in wealth and rise in councils of state, always hovering in the background was the possibility of that midnight knock on the door, with potential loss of property, imprisonment, and even death to follow.

In the early fourth century, though, the winds shifted. In 311, Emperor Galerius issued an edict of toleration in the name of all four members of the ruling tetrarchy of imperial leaders that persecution of Christians should cease.[2] Two years later, emperors Constantine and Licinius legalized Christianity as an accepted faith. The famous story that Constantine did so after seeing a vision of the cross in 312 at the battle of Milvian Bridge may be questionable, and his statement did not make Christianity the empire's official religion—that would not happen until 380 under a different emperor, Theodosius. But Constantine's interest in Christianity was almost certainly genuine, and his actions set his new faith on a new path. This hinge point of Christian history is a very good place to start our story.

A CELEBRATION OR A FUNERAL?

Some years ago, when I was a seminary professor, I had a student in one of my church history classes who, though he was finishing the seminary master's degree he had started, was no longer a Christian. He had great admiration for the scrappy, persecuted, miracle-working New Testament church, but he argued that Christianity had always been intended to be illegal. Constantine's acceptance, he said, had fundamentally changed the character of what Jesus had started, and he could no longer believe in a faith that had ever supported worldly empires. At Milan, he said, Christianity had died.

It's more complicated than that—especially because I believe God can work with the church's choices whether or not they were the best possible choices. Nevertheless, it is true that what happened in the early fourth century fundamentally altered many things about how the faith spread and was practiced. To see how, we have to step back to the beginning.

Our first source for the spread of Christianity—"the Way," as its earliest adherents called it (Acts 9:1-2)—is the Bible itself. The book of Acts begins where the Gospel of Luke ended, telling how Jesus ascended to heaven and the Holy Spirit came upon his disciples as they were gathered in Jerusalem for the Jewish holiday called Shavuot, the Feast of Weeks—in Greek, "Pentecost." The resulting preaching of the gospel by Peter led to over three thousand converts baptized that day, according to Acts 2:41.

The rest of the book of Acts details how the early church spread; how persecution dogged it from both Jewish and Roman sources once it became clear that the Way was no longer a sect of Judaism (which was a protected religion under Roman law); how it received explicit commission to spread among the Gentiles (Acts 10); and how one of its most fervent persecutors, Saul, became its most tireless missionary, Paul.[3] Much of the rest of the New Testament consists of the letters Paul wrote as he traveled, preached, and planted churches—quite a few of which still exist today. Around AD 40, the growing number of believers first acquired the name "Christians" (Χριστιανός), ones who followed Christ.[4] Urban areas seem to have heard the message first, as the apostles and those who came after them sailed from port to port: in these "bustling urban crossroads akin to modern airport hubs," they found ready audience among the "educated, employed and cosmopolitan—the sort of folk who welcomed the open exchange of ideas about everything, including religion."[5]

By the end of the first century, many scholars think the Christian movement numbered around fifty thousand adherents and had spread through the empire to establish itself in forty to fifty cities.[6] It would spread eventually through Asia Minor, Greece, Macedonia, North Africa, Italy; as far as Gaul (modern France) and Spain; and even outside of the Roman Empire's borders to Syria and—if tradition is correct—India.

People were drawn to the faith for a variety of reasons. They marveled at the signs and wonders performed by the early apostles and the respect Christianity gave to those whom Roman society looked down on, such as slaves and women. They appreciated the way that many Christians dedicated themselves to care of the poor and sick since Greek and Roman "public officials did not believe they had any responsibility to prevent disease or to treat those who suffered from it."[7] Consequently, they wanted to join the thick bonds of community established among those early followers. By the middle of the third century, Christians made up 2 percent of the empire's population of sixty million people. By the time of Constantine, they would constitute around 12 percent of the population, and by the beginning of the sixth century there may have been thirty million Christians—pretty much all of the population of the now-declining empire.[8]

ABANDONING TRADITIONAL GODS

But of course, not everyone heard the message gladly. Christians were criticized for being cannibals because they referred to eating Christ's body and blood in the Eucharist (Jn 6:51-59; 1 Cor 11:23-26); promiscuous practitioners of orgies because women and men met together in worship and practiced the kiss of peace (Rom 16:16); superstitious; aggressive in spreading their faith; and, perhaps most damaging from the Roman state's perspective, atheists who sought to overthrow the state:

> The point of such accusations was not that Christians did not believe in a deity, but that they did not believe in and serve the gods who were most deserving of worship—the traditional gods of Rome, who had for centuries guided the Roman people and made their empire great. When asked why they refused to participate in rites that others regarded as little more than patriotic recognition of the state's gods, Christians explained that they could acknowledge no god but their own.[9]

Early persecution of Christians was more sporadic than we sometimes picture, but in the places and times where it flared up, it was severe. In Tertullian's (c. 155–c. 240) *Apology*, written a little before 200, he famously remarked that "the blood of the martyrs is the seed of the church."[10] The early church certainly treasured its martyr stories, retelling them and holding them up as examples. The first great persecution occurred under Nero, as a result of a fire in the year 64. The Christians had not set the fire, but they were blamed for it. Some fifty years after the event, Roman historian Tacitus wrote of the punishments:

> Besides being put to death they were made to serve as objects of amusement; they were clad in the hides of beasts and torn to death by dogs; others were crucified, others set on fire to serve to illuminate the night when daylight failed.[11]

Church historian Eusebius wrote in the early fourth century: "It is related that in [Nero's] reign Paul was beheaded in Rome itself and that Peter was also crucified."[12] Tacitus's narrative implies that most of those killed were poor and were not Roman citizens, who would not have been allowed to be executed in the ways he describes.

The next persecution occurred under Domitian in the 90s. Eusebius claims:

> With terrible cruelty Domitian put to death without trial great numbers of men at Rome who were distinguished by family and career, and without cause banished many other notables and confiscated their property. . . . Tradition has it that the apostle and evangelist John was still alive at this time and was condemned to live on the island of Patmos for his testimony to the divine Word.[13]

In the second century, correspondence between the emperor Trajan and his governor Pliny around 112 gives us our earliest evidence of the way Christian cases were handled in court, as Pliny reported to his superior:

> I have observed the following procedure: I interrogated these as to whether they were Christians; those who confessed I

interrogated a second and a third time, threatening them with punishment; those who persisted I ordered executed.[14]

Hadrian, who reigned from 117 to 138, issued a rescript that protected Christians, but this peace did not last. Significant local persecutions occurred under Marcus Aurelius (who ruled 161–180) and the emperors of the Severan dynasty (r. 193–235). Christians were also criticized regularly in treatises by Greek and Roman writers, and mob violence took place in several places, including Greece and Gaul. One of the most famous martyrs from this era was Polycarp, martyred sometime around 155. An account of his martyrdom, believed to be from a letter written shortly after his death, records the story:

> The Proconsul . . . tried to persuade him to apostatize, saying, "Have respect for your old age, swear by the fortune of Caesar. Repent, and say, 'Down with the Atheists!'" Polycarp looked grimly at the wicked heathen multitude in the stadium, and gesturing towards them, he said, "Down with the Atheists!" "Swear," urged the Proconsul, "reproach Christ, and I will set you free." "86 years have I have served him," Polycarp declared, "and he has done me no wrong. How can I blaspheme my King and my Savior?"[15]

Another of the early church's most famous martyrs, Perpetua, died along with a number of companions in 203 during the reign of Severus. Before she died, she recorded some of her visions, making her the first known female Christian author. These visions were later collected and circulated along with an account of her death (which may have been written by Tertullian). Just before her execution, she wrote of a dream she had about entering the arena:

> And the people began to shout, and my helpers began to sing. And I went up to the master of gladiators and received

the branch. And he kissed me and said to me: "Daughter, peace be with you." And I began to go with glory to the gate called the Gate of Life. And I awoke; and I understood that I should fight, not with beasts but against the devil; but I knew that mine was the victory.[16]

THE GREAT PERSECUTIONS

The next—and perhaps greatest—wave of persecution came under Decius (r. 249–251). In response to perceived military and economic decline, he ordered that anyone who lived in the empire should make a yearly sacrifice to the pagan gods, and he had leading Christians seized. People who sacrificed received a certificate stating they had "poured a libation and sacrificed and eaten some of the sacrificial meat."[17] Many Christians either fled during this persecution or performed the sacrifices; this would cause deep divisions in the church regarding whether to readmit those who had lapsed from the faith and sacrificed. There were two types of offenders here: *sacrificati*, who had actually sacrificed, and *libellatici*, who had not sacrificed but who had bought forged certificates saying they had done so.

The controversy centered on North Africa, where Cyprian, bishop of Carthage, fled into exile and directed church affairs through letters he sent back to his churches. Some of the priests under his care favored readmitting the "lapsed" if they sincerely repented; others thought that apostatizing could never be forgiven. Schism ensued, and a council was finally called to discuss this at Eastertide in 251. The council agreed to readmit believers after they performed penances but would not allow lapsed clergy to resume functioning as clergy. Cyprian's address to the council has survived as the treatise *On the Unity of the Catholic Church*:

If you leave the Church of Christ you will not come to Christ's rewards; you will be an alien, an outcast, an enemy. You cannot have God for your father unless you have the Church for your mother. If you could escape outside Noah's ark, you could escape outside the Church. . . . Nor can he be reckoned as a bishop, who, succeeding to no one, and despising the evangelical and apostolic tradition, sprang from himself. For he who has not been ordained in the Church can neither have nor hold to the Church in any way.[18]

Cyprian lost, however, on the matter of whether baptisms performed by those in schism were valid. Stephen, bishop of Rome, argued that any baptism in the name of the Trinity was valid and appealed to his position as the successor of Peter in support of his arguments—one of the first examples of this argument. In the early fourth century, controversy over the lapsed would break out again.

Meanwhile, Decius had died in 251, and after several other forgettable short-reigning emperors, Valerian came to the throne in 253. He ruled until 260, and his initial toleration of Christianity soon changed to strong persecution. Churches were closed and then confiscated, bishops and clergy executed, and any Christians who served in the imperial government (such Christians were called *Caesariani*) were made slaves.[19] Cyprian, who had already gone into exile during the Decian persecution, was arrested and brought before authorities, who told him:

You have set yourself up as an enemy of the Roman Gods and of their sacred rites. And the pious and most religious emperors . . . have been unable to bring you back to the observance of their own sacred rituals. Therefore . . . you will be executed.[20]

Cyprian was indeed executed in 258.

After Valerian died in 260, the church entered another period of peace. For four decades—though arrests still happened and the educated elite found plenty to criticize in Christian thought and practice—clergy came out of hiding, churches were built, and people practiced their faith in relative peace. But it was the calm before the last great storm.

Diocletian came to the throne in 284 as a result of a coup. He, his co-emperor Maximian, and their assistant emperors (or *caesars*), Constantius and Galerius, attempted to return to the glory days of Rome; Galerius was particularly convinced that Christians were at the root of the empire's troubles. The governing bureaucracy was standardized, currency and prices were made uniform, and Christians were turned out of the civil service and army. When the oracle of the shrine of Apollo complained about the Christians, the four emperors decided to launch a campaign against them.

At first, with Diocletian in charge, bloodshed was avoided, but churches were closed. Many people handed over copies of the Scriptures, which were now illegal to possess. Any Christians who remained among the empire's elite were removed from their positions. Clergy were imprisoned for refusing to sacrifice to the Roman gods. Then in 304, Diocletian got sick. Galerius took over and decreed that every believer, lay or clergy, should sacrifice on pain of death: "The number of martyrs increased, as did the defiance of the Christians."[21]

Although no one realized it then, this was the beginning of the end. In 305, Diocletian and Maximian abdicated in favor of their caesars. Galerius, who reigned in the East, continued to persecute, but his efforts were less and less effective, and in 311 on his deathbed he revoked all his edicts. In the West, Constantius took no further action. In 306 he died, and his army acclaimed his son his successor.

That son's name was Constantine.

"A HYMN TO CHRIST AS TO A GOD"

What did the persecuted church look like at this world-changing moment? When Pliny wrote to Trajan in the early second century, he not only made sure he was conforming to the correct procedure for persecution, he gave us a brief description of Christian life together:

> They asserted, however, that the sum and substance of their fault or error had been that they were accustomed to meet on a fixed day before dawn and sing responsively a hymn to Christ as to a god, and to bind themselves by oath, not to some crime, but not to commit fraud, theft, or adultery, not falsify their trust, nor to refuse to return a trust when called upon to do so. When this was over, it was their custom to depart and to assemble again to partake of food—but ordinary and innocent food. Even this, they affirmed, they had ceased to do after my edict by which, in accordance with your instructions, I had forbidden political associations. Accordingly, I judged it all the more necessary to find out what the truth was by torturing two female slaves who were called deaconesses. But I discovered nothing else but depraved, excessive superstition.[22]

Broadly speaking, Pliny had gotten the right idea; the earliest documents that give us a picture of Christian life and worship sound a lot like his description.[23] Of course customs varied from place to place, and not everyone always lived up to the high ideals put forward in these early church orders. But the most famous of these manuscripts give us a picture of a community that saw itself as distinct from the world, centered itself around weekly meetings for worship and prayer and the Eucharist, concerned itself with church discipline, and was dedicated to serving those whom Roman society ignored, including placing women and slaves in positions of leadership.

In a Roman home, women and slaves had their place, and all the family's activities were subject to the *paterfamilias*, the family's head—he could even sell his own children as slaves if he chose. In some times and places, women could not even appear in public.[24] One scholar notes, "The stratification of Roman society was tight and stiff and minute. In a world obsessed with status and snobbery, and with their symbols and ethics and laws, everyone knew his place, and it was an offense (*contumacia*) not to show deference to those who were above you."[25] But in the Christian community slaves and free, citizens and immigrants could all worship together. Paul's letter to the churches in Galatia is radical now, but it was even more radical then: "As many of you as were baptized into Christ have clothed yourselves with Christ. There is no longer Jew or Greek, there is no longer slave or free, there is no longer male and female; for all of you are one in Christ Jesus" (Gal 3:27-28).

Soon the church's ecclesiastical government began to coalesce around the figure of the bishop, who was in charge of the church or churches in a city and had presbyters (those ordained to the ministry of Word and sacrament), deacons, and lay believers under his care. Gradually, it developed a New Testament canon to go with the Scriptures it shared with Judaism, now commonly called by Christians the Old Testament. By the year 200, the four Gospels and Paul's letters were unambiguously considered Scripture, and by the fourth century we have a New Testament list that matches our modern one. We will speak more in the next chapter of the way the church began to delineate its defining doctrines, as it built on its experience of the life, death, and resurrection of Jesus and argued against pagan and heretical ways of worship and belief. Here, we want to look at its communal life.

The Didache (often called the Teaching of the Twelve Apostles) is usually dated to the late first century and gives a set of instructions for living the life of the Way. It reminds Christians that there are "two ways, one of life and one of death,"[26] and instructs followers of the way of life that they should follow the Ten Commandments; avoid other sins; avoid food offered to idols; fast "on the fourth day and on the Preparation," as opposed to "hypocrites" who fasted on other days;[27] serve the poor; be hospitable to traveling prophets and other believers; and await the second coming. They should rule their common life by appointing "bishops and deacons worthy of the Lord"; and they should meet every Lord's Day to "gather yourselves together, and break bread, and give thanksgiving after having confessed your transgressions, that your sacrifice may be pure."[28] The Didache also includes prayers to be said at Communion and instructions for baptism:

> Baptize into the name of the Father, and of the Son, and of the Holy Spirit, in living water. But if you have no living water, baptize into other water; and if you cannot do so in cold water, do so in warm. But if you have neither, pour out water three times upon the head into the name of Father and Son and Holy Spirit.[29]

In about the year 150, Justin Martyr (100–165) put forth a similar description in his *First Apology*, which was written to argue to the elites and the emperor of his day (Antonius Pius) against the persecution of Christians. To combat the slanders that often arose when people misunderstood Christian worship, Justin Martyr described it. His description is worth quoting at length:

> On the day called Sunday there is a gathering together in the same place of all who live in a given city or rural district. The memoirs of the apostles or the writings of the prophets

are read, as long as time permits. Then when the reader ceases, the president in a discourse admonishes and urges the imitation of these good things. Next we all rise together and send up prayers. When we cease from our prayer, bread is presented and wine and water. The president in the same manner sends up prayers and thanksgivings, according to his ability, and the people sing out their assent, saying the "Amen."

A distribution and participation of the elements for which thanks have been given is made to each person, and to those who are not present they are sent by the deacons. Those who have means and are willing, each according to his own choice, gives what he wills, and what is collected is deposited with the president. He provides for the orphans and widows, those who are in need on account of sickness or some other cause, those who are in bonds, strangers who are sojourning, and in a word he becomes the protector of all who are in need. We all make our assembly in common on Sunday, since it is the first day, on which God changed the darkness and matter and made the world, and Jesus Christ our Savior arose from the dead on the same day.[30]

Jumping forward almost another century, we next encounter a document called *The Apostolic Tradition*, traditionally attributed to an important theologian in Rome named Hippolytus (170–235). It shows a church with growing need for structure as it records instructions for ordaining bishops, elders, and deacons—and what to do about other groups of people with various callings, for example:

The reader is appointed when the bishop gives the book to him. He does not have hands laid upon him. . . . Hands are not laid on a virgin, for a decision alone makes her a virgin. . . . If someone among the laity is seen to have received a gift of healing by revelation, hands are not laid upon such a one, for the matter is obvious.[31]

The Apostolic Tradition also describes what to do when someone wants to become a Christian—prescribing a much longer period of instruction and preparation than the Didache, which had recommended only several days of fasting—and outlines a beautiful baptismal liturgy to be used at the vigil service the night before Easter Sunday to welcome them. It gives various other regulations regarding how often to pray (at the third, sixth, and ninth hours and at bedtime, midnight, and dawn) and how often to fast (frequently) and explains how the bishop conducts evening prayer and blesses the community's common meal. Perhaps the most beautiful set of instructions are those for prayer at midnight:

> For those elders who handed down the tradition to us taught us that in this hour every creature hushes for a brief moment to praise the Lord. Stars and trees and waters stand still for an instant. All the host of angels serving him, together with the souls of the righteous, praise God.[32]

IN THIS SIGN CONQUER?

Not all of these things would change when Constantine legalized Christianity, and not everything that would change would do so immediately. But his story forms an important bridge—in more ways than one.[33]

Constantine was born around 272 in Naissus, in an area now part of modern-day Serbia, the son of a "barmaid and a young army officer," as one historian memorably puts it.[34] His father was Illyrian; his mother, Greek. His mother, Helena, converted to Christianity, probably before Constantine was born and certainly before he converted; she may have done so in response to a plague around 270. His father, Constantinus Chlorus, rose in the military quickly and around 282 became governor of Dalmatia and in 288 praetorian prefect—a high-ranking aide to the emperor. At that time, Chlorus divorced Helena (if in fact they were ever legally married) and contracted a marriage with Theodora, daughter of Maximian, who had recently become Roman emperor in the West; Diocletian had begun a policy of dividing the empire into Eastern and Western halves, each ruled over by co-emperors.[35]

Constantine and his mother went to live in the court of Diocletian. In 293, Diocletian created a tetrarchy whereby each half of the empire was ruled by an *augustus* (a senior emperor) and a *caesar* (a junior emperor). Emperor Maximian promoted Constantine's father (now Maximian's son-in-law) to become his caesar. Constantine also received a promotion to military tribune, a rank often seen as a precursor to a political career. His campaigns won him renown, and we know that he accompanied Diocletian on some of them. In 305, an agreement was made that Diocletian and Maximian would retire, that Constantinus Chlorus and Galerius (the caesar in the East) would be promoted to *augusti*, and that Constantine and Maximian's son Maxentius would become caesars. But Galerius succeeded in having two of his friends promoted to caesar instead. Constantine joined his father, who was fighting in Gaul and Britain, and there was proclaimed augustus when his father died in 306—though he quickly announced to Galerius that he was happy to be "only" a caesar. In 307, though, he was unambiguously proclaimed augustus of the West.

This did not end his troubles. A series of civil wars followed—at one point in 310, there were five emperors of one rank or another all claiming to be part of the tetrarchy. The odd man out was Maxentius, son of Maximian, and it was his army that Constantine was fighting at Milvian Bridge.

"In the summer of 312," writes a historian, "Constantine invaded Italy with an army inferior in number to Maxentius's but with better training. And in probably the most pivotal decision in Roman history, Constantine placed himself and his forces under the protection of the Christian God."[36] Why did he do this?

Roman historian Lactantius said that Constantine had a dream the night before the battle that told him to mark a Christian sign on the shields of his soldiers; Eusebius added to this account of the dream that Christ appeared to Constantine and told him to mark a *Chi Rho* (the two Greek letters that begin the word *Christos* in Greek, like this: ☧) on the army's standard. Furthermore, Eusebius said in his *Life of Constantine*—claiming he had the story straight from the emperor himself—that while marching toward battle a vision had burst upon Constantine's eyes of "a trophy of the cross arising from the light of the sun, carrying the message Conquer By This."[37]

Constantine was not at this point a Christian, but in all probability his mother was, and he was known to be a protector of Christians as his father had been. He certainly had what could be described as a monotheistic devotion to the Sun God Sol, or Apollo. He questioned Christian clergy who traveled with him about the meaning of the symbol in the vision. From them he learned the symbolism of the cross, and the next day he indeed had the *Chi-Rho* symbol put onto his battle standard, along with "a bar holding a banner with the imperial portrait," and instructed his soldiers to mark it on their shields.[38] The newly christened army reached Rome, where Maxentius was holed up, in October. After a pagan oracle told Maxentius that "the enemy of the Roman people would perish on that day," he confidently marched out to meet Constantine. But Maxentius was the one who was defeated by Constantine on October 28, 312.[39]

Freedom at Last

Much ink has been spilled over whether Constantine actually converted to worshiping the God of the Christians at this moment. He delayed baptism until his deathbed, but this was common at the time.[40] There is strong evidence that he considered himself to be devoted to the Christian God after the events of Milvian Bridge; he even eventually issued coinage with Christian symbols rather than those honoring Sol/Apollo. And there is no doubt that nine months later he met with Licinius (augustus of the East) at Milan and that they agreed on an edict proclaiming "full toleration for all religions as well as restitution for Christians."[41] It reads in part:

> No one whatsoever should be denied the opportunity to give his heart to the observance of the Christian religion, of that religion which he should think best for himself, so that the Supreme Deity . . . may show in all things His usual favor and benevolence. Therefore, your Worship should know that . . . [anyone] who wishes to observe Christian religion may do so freely and openly, without molestation.[42]

How this changed the church and the empire to which it was proclaimed will, in part, be the tale of our next chapter. However, it is worth noting one irony that pastor and historian Peter Leithart points out in his biography of Constantine. When the emperor was baptized during what he correctly surmised to be his last illness, Eusebius tells us that Constantine put off his purple robes—symbol of his earthly power—and refused to wear them again; he instead "arrayed himself in shining imperial vestments, brilliant as the light, and reclined on a couch of the purest white."[43]

Constantine told the clergy assembled that if he survived his illness he planned to devote himself *now* to service to the church, not the state: "As Eusebius recounted the story, Constantine seemed to believe there was a basic incompatibility between being an emperor and being a Christian, between court and church, warfare and prayer, the purple and the white."[44]

So, too, my formerly Christian student thought. Whether he and Constantine were right has been a matter of debate within the church ever since.

Recommended Reading

Brown, Peter. *The World of Late Antiquity*. New York: Norton, 1971.

Clark, Elizabeth. *Women in the Early Church*. Wilmington, DE: Glazier, 1983.

Dupont, Florence. *Daily Life in Ancient Rome*. Oxford: Blackwell, 2008.

Frederikson, Paula. *When Christians Were Jews*. New Haven, CT: Yale University Press, 2019.

Jeffers, James S. *Conflict at Rome*. Minneapolis: Fortress, 1991.

Leithart, Peter. *Defending Constantine: The End of an Empire and the Dawn of Christendom*. Downers Grove, IL: InterVarsity Press, 2010.

Papandrea, James. *A Week in the Life of Rome*. Downers Grove, IL: InterVarsity Press, 2019.

Stephenson, Paul. *Constantine: Roman Emperor, Christian Victor*. New York: Overlook, 2007.

two

THE NICENE CREED (325)

*"Light from Light, true God from true God,
begotten not made, of one substance
with the Father."*

Somewhere in the world, every Sunday, in some church, someone is saying those words. Someone has been saying them somewhere every Sunday for over sixteen hundred years. They may be saying them in Greek or Latin or English or French or Arabic or Old Church Slavonic; they may be repeating them as part of a very simple order of worship or an ornately constructed liturgy; but someone somewhere is repeating those words.

Why? To tell that story, we must first resume the story of Constantine legalizing and adopting the Christian faith. He began to worry about the content of that faith and the divisions and disagreements among those who professed it. This led him to call a council that was meant to involve all parts of the Christian church as it stood in the early fourth century. All 1800 bishops of the church were invited, though only about 250 to 300 actually attended.[1] They met in the city of Nicaea along the shores of a lake in the province of Bithynia. Today the place is called İznik and is part of Turkey. Already the young church was professing the triune God in its liturgies and prayers while also confessing belief in a Christ who was fully human and fully divine. At Nicaea the church began to define clearly how they could mean both.[2]

Son of Man and Son of God

Some years ago, my husband was traveling on an airplane and was seated next to a Muslim passenger. My husband was friendly and wished to talk, and so was his seatmate. They spoke courteously to each other about their respective faiths. At one point they were speaking of the life of Jesus and the fact that Christians believe Jesus to be divine *and* human. My husband's new acquaintance turned to him and said, "That is one thing I do not understand about Christians. If Jesus was truly a man, he had to go to the bathroom. You worship a God who went to the bathroom."

In that moment, my husband said, he understood the words he had said his whole life about Jesus being fully human and fully divine in a new way. If Jesus was truly human, he shared all the parts of our existence—hunger, fear, sadness, thirst, and, yes, even going to the bathroom. He was a baby who needed his diaper changed and a young man whose finger hurt when he hit it with a tool in the carpenter's shop. He had friends desert him and betray him, and he had family members who died. He felt every moment of his crucified pain.

"Yes," my husband said. "*That's* why I'm a Christian. I believe in a God who can go to the bathroom."

They didn't put it in those words, but that, in a nutshell, was what the Council of Nicaea, and the Councils of Constantinople and Chalcedon that refined its teaching, were about. The writings that became the New Testament, Christian hymns, and liturgies had all testified for over three hundred years that Jesus was truly human and truly divine, but at Nicaea the church stated what it meant *theologically* when it affirmed this. In fact, it said that to believe otherwise was outside the bounds of Christian belief:

> But those who say: "There was a time when he was not"; and "He was not before he was made"; and "He was made out of nothing," or "He is of another substance" or "essence," or "The Son of God is created," or "changeable," or "alterable"—they are condemned by the holy catholic and apostolic Church.[3]

How did this debate arise? In order to understand that, we have to begin to think about not only what the early church practiced but what it taught. As the young movement grew, leaders arose. Some were bishops and priests; others laymen and in a few cases laywomen, like Perpetua. Probably there were many more laywomen than we know about, but their testimonies were not always written down or preserved.

Collectively, we refer to these leaders as the church fathers and mothers. They were known for their ecclesiastical leadership, their theological and apologetic writings that defended Christianity in the face of pagan opposition, and sometimes for their violent deaths as martyrs. Through their lives and writings, they passed on the faith that we know today: faith in a Savior who came to be understood as truly human and truly divine, whose death on the cross dealt with the sins of humanity, who had been resurrected and ascended to the Father, and who would someday return.

How We Got Our Bible

The earliest writings that we have from the young Christian movement now make up the pages of our New Testament. Paul's letters were written to encourage churches in the face of persecution and hardship and to give instructions and mediate disputes, and they were likely composed between AD 50 and 65. The four Gospels—stories of Jesus' life composed for different audiences—and Acts—written by the author of Luke to take the story past the resurrection and the ascension—are known to have existed by the last decade of the first century.

But how did we get these writings all collected together into the New Testament? Churches began to circulate copies of these books and others that they found helpful: letters by other leaders such as Peter and James and the apocalyptic writing known as the Revelation to John. They also circulated copies of other books. For example, some people passed around infancy narratives of Christ's childhood and a set of sayings referred to as the Gospel of Thomas.

Also shared were the writings of a number of church leaders whom we call today the Apostolic Fathers because they lived so close to the time of the apostles—Clement of Rome (c. 35–99), Ignatius of Antioch (c. 35–c. 107), Polycarp (69–155), the author of the epistle of Barnabas (we don't know his real name), and the Shepherd of Hermas (we don't know his real name either) as well as the Didache, which was introduced in chapter one.[4] A number of these writings encouraged Christians in times of hardship and persecution, and they gave instructions on various practical matters. By the year 150, as historian Joseph Lienhard notes, the church

> exhibited many features that would mark it for centuries: Christians baptized in the name of the Father, Son, and Holy Spirit; they celebrated the Lord's Supper weekly; they were governed by a bishop, presbyters, and deacons. But they still lacked one thing that would become central to Christian identity: a New Testament. Their only Holy Scripture was that collection of sacred writings later called

the Old Testament, which they generally read in the "Septuagint" version—a Greek translation pre-dating Jesus by over a century.[5]

Many of the books circulated among churches contained valuable information and spiritual guidance. But some expressed heretical views. A consensus as to which books were valuable and which were heretical began to arise, but there was no single approved list.

How long would this situation have lasted if conflict had not arisen? We don't know. But there was a conflict. About the year 140, Marcion of Sinope (c. 85–160), a wealthy layman, was excommunicated from the church at Rome and founded his own church. Marcion believed "that the god of the Old Testament was an inferior god, the creator and judge, distinct from the God of love who was the Father of Jesus Christ."[6] He prepared his own list of approved books, which included the epistles of Paul and the Gospel of Luke with Old Testament references removed.

In response to Marcion as well as to other controversies, truly authoritative lists of books began to appear. Irenaeus of Lyons (c. 120–c. 200) was "the first Christian writer to use, as Scripture, almost all the books that are in our New Testament today."[7] He insisted that these books could be properly used only by those people who accepted four authorities:

1. The "rule . . . of truth"; that is, the belief in one God, one Son, and one Holy Spirit, the basis of the later creeds.

2. The whole canonical body of Scripture, Old and New.

3. The apostolic tradition; that is, the deposit handed down, once for all, by the apostles and preserved intact in the church to the present.

4. The bishops whose very lives as direct successors to the apostles provided the church with a visible witness that the true teaching about Christ was still being preserved and preached.[8]

By about the year 200, the mainstream of Christians accepted all four Gospels, Acts, all the letters traditionally believed to have been written by Paul, and 1 Peter and 1 John. But what was the standard by which orthodox faith—and which books were orthodox—should be judged? Before the word *canon* was used to refer to the books of the Bible, it was used to refer to what was also known as the "rule of faith" or the "rule of truth."[9] Irenaeus of Lyons had named it as his standard, and he described orthodox Christian faith as belief in:

> God the Father, uncreated, beyond grasp, invisible, one God the maker of all; . . . the Word of God, the Son of God, Christ Jesus our Lord, who was shown forth by the prophets according to the design of their prophecy and according to the manner in which the Father established; and through him were made all things entirely. . . . He became a man among men, visible and tangible, in order to abolish death and bring to light life and bring about communion of God and man. And the third is the Holy Spirit, through whom the prophets prophesied . . . and who in the end of times has been poured forth in a new manner upon humanity over all the earth renewing man to God.[10]

All the variations on this rule that we know of shared a confession of God as triune and of Jesus as the one who had been born, died, resurrected, and ascended. Many of those who made their name as Christian writers in the church's first three centuries were those who defended this common faith either against pagans or against the heresy of Gnosticism.

Gnosticism was a diverse movement, but one centered on the belief that matter was evil and created by some lesser evil creator, the god of the Old Testament, who had fallen out with the true God. For Gnostics, Christ provided salvation not through death on the cross (he had only *appeared* to die) but through secret knowledge that he gave to his true disciples. Against the Gnostic background, the question of a Jesus who had really lived as a human being and yet was also the God who had created the universe—not some lesser being or emanation— became increasingly acute.

SINGING IN THE STREETS

So how did the controversy that led directly to Nicaea begin? Alexander, archbishop of Alexandria (d. 326), had been a disciple of renowned scholar and exegete Origen of Alexandria (c. 185–c. 254) and shared his emphasis on Christ as the eternal *Logos* or Word, drawing from scriptural sources such as John 1. In his writings, Alexander began to emphasize the eternal time- lessness of the Son, "born not created, God from God, Light from Light, True God from true God"; Alexander "wanted to distinguish clearly between Christian and pagan theology by ar- guing that divinity is an absolute term."[11]

One of the priests in his diocese, Arius, was bothered by Alexander's position. "Like many heretics," one historian notes, Arius "began by trying not to be one."[12] He wanted to avoid her- esies of his day that called the Son either "an emanation" from the Father or simply a part of the Father, and he too was a dis- ciple of Origen. But he felt that Origen's emphasis on the ab- solute primacy of God the Father meant that the Son could not be timeless in the same way, and he famously stated: "There was a time when the Son was not."[13]

Arius believed that Alexander was attacking Christianity's claim to be a monotheistic faith. What is more, Arius thought he had Scripture on his side, pointing to such verses as Mark 10:18. Arius taught his slogans about the issue to his parishioners, and soon the debate was sweeping the city in everything from graffiti to popular songs. Alexander knew a public relations crisis when he saw one, and he deposed and censured Arius—promptly creating an even bigger public relations crisis because Arius appealed to Bishop Eusebius of Nicomedia, who was a distant relation of Emperor Constantine.[14]

Meanwhile, Constantine had been consolidating his control over the empire. In 313 he had cooperated with the augustus of the East, Licinius, in issuing the Edict of Milan; by 323 he was battling Licinius for supremacy—and winning. He fought explicitly as "the Christian champion against an enemy who put his trust in Jupiter."[15] After defeating Licinius, he moved his capital city from Rome to Byzantium in the East and renamed it after himself—Constantinople. By this point, it was almost twenty years since he had first taken power, and he determined that in 325 the anniversary would be celebrated with all due pomp. If only his Eastern bishops weren't embroiled in such a large dispute! So he summoned them all together to settle their differences.

The bishops first gathered on June 19, 325. Constantine opened the council by accepting petitions from the bishops, then promptly burned them all and said that "the debts of all had been canceled."[16] In addition to the big theological dispute, there were many smaller items to be settled. The council decided in favor of the Western method of celebrating Easter—on a Sunday, the day of the Resurrection—rather than the Eastern method of celebrating it on the Jewish month and day of Nisan 14, when Passover was celebrated.[17] They also defeated a proposal to enforce celibacy on members of the clergy, though clergy could not marry after ordination, and one of the twenty canons (rules) put forth by the council stated that "no woman is to live in the home of unmarried clergy, except for a mother, sister, or aunt."[18]

The other canons all addressed other issues that were highly practical in early-fourth-century culture. Eunuchs were allowed to become clergy unless they had made themselves eunuchs; bishops had to be chosen by other bishops; Rome, Alexandria, and Antioch were to be considered the highest-ranking sees (seats of bishops); and regulations were issued that dealt with ordination and with various kinds of heretics and with those who had lapsed during persecution. Furthermore, converts must undergo probation before holding an office in the church; clergy should not try to exercise authority outside their own areas; deacons should not try to administer the Eucharist; no clergy should lend money at interest; bishops' decisions to excommunicate should be respected by other bishops; and "for the sake of uniformity in the church, on the Lord's Day and Pentecost all should pray standing rather than kneeling."[19]

But the big-ticket item was undoubtedly the theological question posed by Arius and Alexander. It probably surprised no one that Arius presented his position partially in the same chants and songs he had taught his parishioners. However, those bishops present who possessed the most theological training were largely in favor of the Alexandrian position.

The council appears to have sought out examples of local creeds used in baptism that confessed the "rule of faith" discussed above. By this time Bishop Eusebius of Caesarea, who backed Arius, had been deposed for his part in the controversy, but Constantine pressured the Council of Nicaea to restore him to office. Eusebius offered the baptismal creed of Jerusalem as a pattern for a statement by the council. This didn't actually address the issue in precise enough language to rule out the Arian position, so the bishops decided to add commentary clarifying the relationship of the Son and the Father. They used Alexander's earlier language about "God from God," but they also insisted on the inclusion of the Greek word *homoousios*, "of the same substance": "If the Logos was *homoousios* with the Father, he was truly God alongside the Father."[20]

Many of the bishops supported this statement, but not all. The Arian party criticized it for a number of reasons, perhaps the strongest one being that the word was "not found in the Holy Scriptures."[21] Nevertheless, it made it into the creed that was issued, and *anathemas* were added to the end of the creed against the Arian position. Arius was excommunicated. The council ended after seven weeks with the holding of a great banquet.[22] Constantine thought his public relations disaster was over. In truth, it had just started.

NICAEA TO CONSTANTINOPLE TO CHALCEDON

Part of the reason the debate went on was, ironically, Constantine himself. Though he had called Arius "a god of war who seeks to create strife and violence" during the council, the emperor was willing to consider Arius's petitions for reinstatement (which continued until Arius died in 336) and eventually became convinced that Arius's thoughts were, in fact, within the bounds of orthodox belief.[23] Constantine's son, Constantinus, who explicitly supported the Arian position, criticized, deposed, and exiled Nicaea-supporting bishops. This was also the case with several further successors until the reign of Theodosius from 379 to 395.

Another reason the debate continued was because no one actually expected it to resolve the issue. The council's canons were binding, but the creed was not one of those canons, though it was certainly a statement of belief made by a large and important group of bishops gathered at the behest of the emperor. As one historian notes:

> Local creeds continued to be used for teaching converts and children until the next century. (One of the best examples is the "Apostles' Creed," which originated as the

local creed of the Roman church.) . . . No one regarded [the
creed of Nicaea] as a universal marker of orthodoxy. At
that point in history, no creed was treated that way.[24]

Nicaea was an important event in the church's attempt to understand the divinity of Christ, but it was part of a larger set of debates about this throughout the fourth century. Heresies the
church rejected around this issue during the fourth and fifth
centuries included Docetism (Christ only appeared to take on a
human body and to die); Apollinarianism (Christ had a divine
mind and will in human flesh); Modalism (God is not truly
triune, but one God who takes on different roles and names);
Ebionitism (Christ was a special prophet); Adoptionism (God
the Father adopted Jesus at his baptism); Monophysitism
(Christ's divinity swallowed up his humanity); and Nestorianism
(Christ has two natures living in two persons within him).[25]

Yet another reason the debate continued had to do with a man
who was a twenty-seven-year-old deacon at the time of Nicaea:
Athanasius. Only three years after the council, Athanasius was
made bishop of the important See of Alexandria. Among other
responsibilities, the bishop of Alexandria was now supposed to
determine the date of Easter, and Athanasius used the opportunity to write circular letters to other bishops in which he put
forth the *homoousian* view: "In a rhetorical masterstroke he presented his enemies as 'Arians' rather than 'Christians.'"[26]

Exiled several times for his beliefs (and quite possibly his over-
bearing management style), Athanasius used the time to
compose the theological treatises we remember him for today,
including the robust confession of Jesus' humanity and divinity
called *On the Incarnation*, written in the 310s. There he expressed
one of the most famous statements of the *homoousian* position
ever penned:

He, indeed, assumed humanity that we might become God. He manifested Himself by means of a body in order that we might perceive the Mind of the unseen Father. He endured shame from men that we might inherit immortality.[27]

Not all of those who held what we would consider today the Arian position would have considered themselves disciples or followers of Arius. In fact, at the time Arius was seen as a *Eusebian*, a follower of both Eusebius of Caesarea and Eusebius of Nicomedia. Both of these bishops disagreed with the doctrine that had been expressed at Nicaea and was continuing to be expressed by the troublesome Athanasius. As the fourth century wore on, a new movement called *homoian* arose among the Eusebians—supported by Constantinus, who was now his father Constantine's sole successor. They argued that the Son was like the Father, but inferior. The most extreme even maintained that he was *unlike* the Father; they became a distinct group who quarreled with the rest of the Eusebians. Constantinus successfully got a council to agree to a *homoian* creed in 360, but the next year he died. His successor, Julian "the Apostate," ruled from 361 to 363 and tried to revive paganism.

In the face of this, support finally coalesced around the Nicene Creed as the one uniform statement of faith that everyone could agree on against the *homoians*. When Theodosius came to the throne, he called the Council of Constantinople in 381. That council affirmed the Nicene Creed as a standard of orthodoxy for the church—though they subtracted the anathemas, added a longer description of the work of the Holy Spirit, and made some other small changes of wording that make the text generally more readable. "In its original form," a historian once said, "the Nicene Creed was a weapon. It was to become a sublime article of faith."[28]

We do not have detailed records of either Nicaea or Constantinople, but in 451 another council, this one held at Chalcedon, preserved the text that had been decided on seventy years earlier at Constantinople. Allowing for small changes of translation, and one major change that we'll discuss in chapter four, this is the version that is confessed in churches today. Arianism was not dead—the Germanic tribes in the north and west of Europe held on to it until the early Middle Ages—but it was dying.

Chalcedon was another in a series of what was now the "time-honored policy of summoning a general council" to deal with doctrinal issues.[29] There would be seven "great councils" in all, which the vast majority of orthodox Christians still recognize as defining for the faith: Nicaea (325), Constantinople (381), Ephesus (431), Chalcedon (451), Constantinople II (553), Constantinople III (680–681), and Nicaea II (787).

It should be noted that a group referred to today as the Oriental Orthodox or non-Chalcedonians—which include Coptic, Ethiopian, Armenian, Syriac, Indian, and Eritrean churches—rejected the agreements about the nature of Christ's divinity that were put forth at Chalcedon. They confess with the rest of orthodox Christianity that Christ is both human and divine, but they argue that he has only one nature, not both a human and a divine nature in one person. These churches continue today, numbering about sixty million members; their tradition is every bit as ancient as the Chalcedonian tradition in which all Western Christians and other Eastern Christians stand, and many have suffered heavy persecution, from the Armenian genocide to modern-day laws restricting Coptic Christianity.

Chalcedon is important for another reason besides its finalization of the creed. There the church rejected Apollinarianism, Monophysitism, and Nestorianism, all ways of describing Christ that struck the wrong balance between divinity and humanity:

Against the earlier heretic Arius, the assembly affirmed that Jesus was truly God, and against Apollinarius that he was truly man. Against Eutyches it confessed that Jesus' deity and humanity were not changed into something else, and against the Nestorians that Jesus was not divided but was one person.[30]

The Chalcedonian Definition, as it is often technically called, is worth quoting at length:

Therefore, following the holy fathers, all of us teach unanimously that everyone must confess that our Lord Jesus Christ is one single and same Son, who is perfect according to divinity and perfect according to humanity,

truly God and truly man, composed of a reasonable [i.e., rational] soul and a body, consubstantial with the Father according to divinity and consubstantial with us according to humanity, completely like us except for sin;

he was begotten by the Father before all ages according to his divinity, and in these latter days, he was born for us and for our salvation of Mary the Virgin, the Mother of God, according to his humanity,

one single and same Christ, Son, Lord, only begotten, known in two natures, without confusion, without change, without division, without separation;

the difference in natures is in no way suppressed by their union, but rather the properties of each are retained and united in one single person and single hypostasis [substance];

he is neither separated nor divided in two persons, but he is a single and same only-begotten Son, God the Word, the Lord Jesus Christ,

such as he was announced formerly by the prophets, such as he himself, the Lord Jesus Christ, taught us about himself, and such as the symbol of the fathers [the Nicene Creed] has transmitted to us.[31]

In this statement, we see an attempt to guard against *all* the heresies that had troubled the earlier church, and to confess a Christ who was fully God, fully human, with two natures in one person. For centuries, it "set the boundaries in which Christians were to think about Jesus Christ."[32]

I Believe in a God Who . . .

Criticism has been leveled against Nicaea and the councils that followed it, not only in their own centuries (the Germanic tribes of Europe adopted Arian Christianity for centuries) but all the way down to our own. The contemporary novel *The Da Vinci Code* enjoyed a brief moment of fame with its inaccurate claim that at Nicaea the bishops took a vote and decided Christ was divine.[33]

A more serious criticism from sincere believers has been that the formation of creeds represents a moment when the church allowed philosophy to hold the Scriptures captive. None of the most important Greek terms used in the debate—like *homoousious,* the term that won the day at Nicaea, or *hypostasis,* the technical term used to describe Christ's two natures in one person at Chalcedon—can be found in Scripture. Arius was clearly able to quote Scripture to support his position.

However, an argument that rejects Nicaea and other creedal statements as pagan philosophy ignores how much the Scriptures were at the heart of the debate. Nicaea—and Constantinople and Chalcedon—bequeathed us a principle of interpretation that united the Scriptures into one overwhelming narrative, from Genesis to Revelation. That narrative is the story of a good God who created and loves the world, who entered that world as a human being to deal with the sin of human beings, who suffered and died and was resurrected, who ascended and would come again at the end of time to usher in a glorious new heaven and a new earth where sin and sorrow would have no place.

Yes, we believe in a God who went to the bathroom—because we believe that God the Son became human, suffered, and died to save us.

RECOMMENDED READING

Anatolios, Khaled. *Retrieving Nicaea*. Grand Rapids, MI: Baker Academic, 2011.

Ayres, Lewis. *Nicaea and Its Legacy*. Oxford: Oxford University Press, 2006.

Behr, John. *The Way to Nicaea*. Crestwood, NY: St. Vladimir's Seminary Press, 2001.

George, Timothy, ed. *Evangelicals and Nicene Faith*. Grand Rapids, MI: Baker Academic, 2011.

Hanson, R. P. C. *The Search for the Christian Doctrine of God*. Grand Rapids, MI: Baker Academic, 2005.

Williams, Rowan. *Arius*. London: SCM, 2001.

Young, Frances M., with Andrew Teal. *From Nicaea to Chalcedon*. 2nd ed. Grand Rapids, MI: Baker Academic, 2010.

three

THE RULE OF SAINT BENEDICT (C. 530)

*"And so we are going to establish a school
for the service of the Lord."*

B enedict of Nursia (c. 480–c. 547) wrote these words almost 1500 years ago in the prologue to what may well be the most famous monastic document ever produced: *The Rule of Saint Benedict.*[1]

Had there been monks before Benedict? Yes. People like Antony of Egypt had sought out an ascetical life ever since martyrdom was no longer a way to show one's devotion after the legalization of the Christian faith. Had monks and nuns gathered together in communities? Yes. The names Pachomius, Basil of Caesarea, Melania, Macrina, Martin of Tours, and John Cassian are all names important to that story, and you'll meet them below. Famed theologians Jerome and Augustine even make cameo appearances. But this wealthy Roman pagan turned solitary ascetic turned leader of thirteen communities, set pen to paper to write a little handbook for those under his care and by doing so became the father of Western monasticism.[2] Benedict's influence on the history of the Western church was profound, and its impact is still being felt today.

WHY MONKS?

In the late 1980s, when I was in college, one of my classes took a field trip to a nearby monastery, New Melleray, near Dubuque, Iowa. While I had heard of the monastic life before, and even read excerpts from some of the great monastic writers in my devotional times, this was the first time I had spent any time in close proximity to a monastery or convent. Some of the monks met with us. We had an opportunity to roam the grounds and to participate in the daily round of worship undertaken by the monks.

If you go to New Melleray's website today, you'll read this description of their mission:

> Disciples of Jesus Christ, we join countless men and women who throughout fifteen hundred years have discovered the *Rule of Saint Benedict* to offer a challenging and effective way of living the Gospel. . . .
>
> Like all monasteries, New Melleray Abbey is a school of charity. The monastery is a place where we learn to love God, to love ourselves, and to love each other. Together with its fertile farmland and rugged woodlands our monastery provides us with solitude and precious silence.[3]

In the early church, too, people were seeking ways to grow closer to God. Before the legalization of Christianity, we see evidence of people and communities devoted to prayer, like the widows praying night and day (1 Tim 5:5). Soon, we also begin to hear stories about men and women going out into the desert to practice a strict and disciplined life.

The most famous of the early ascetics (from ἄσκησις, *askēsis*, Greek for "exercise") was Antony of Egypt (251–356), a young Egyptian man who, inspired by a sermon on Matthew 19:21, gave his belongings to the poor and moved to the desert. Antony had a "brilliant biographer" in Athanasius (from chap. 2), bishop of

Alexandria, one of many "pious publicists" who spread the fame of Antony and other desert fathers and mothers far and wide.[4] When Christians no longer faced state-supported persecution, the number of desert dwellers increased. Among other famed desert *abbas* and *ammas* (Aramaic for "father" and "mother") were Macarius of Egypt (300–391), Moses the Black (330–405), Macrina (c. 330–379), Mary of Egypt (c. 344–c. 421), and Syncletica of Alexandria (d. 350).

While the hermit life attracted many, the idea of gathering to practice spiritual discipline in community was also compelling. Pachomius (292–348) often gets the title of "father of cenobitic monasticism," that is, life in community. He began his life as an ascetic in Egypt but sometime around 320 founded a monastery at Tabennisi. It eventually grew to accommodate more than a hundred monks under the rule of a superior. These monks grew their own food, cared for their own sick (and, during times of trouble, their neighbors' sick, poor, elderly, and orphans as well), and prayed in community.[5] Eventually his movement grew to multiple communities, including several for women, numbering over seven thousand. Around the same time, Bishop Basil of Caesarea (330–379) was also founding communities in Cappadocia and giving them rules for living.[6]

Such community life was particularly attractive to women, for whom it represented an escape from the structures of Roman society that placed them always in relationship to men (husbands, fathers, brothers). In Rome, Jerome (c. 347–420), who had lived for a time as a desert ascetic, developed an advisory relationship with aristocratic Roman widows such as Marcella (325–410) and Paula (347–404), both of whom consecrated their celibate widowhood to God. Paula helped Jerome translate the Bible into Latin from Greek and Hebrew, and when he was exiled from Rome to Bethlehem, she went with him and helped establish communities of both men and women there. Melania the Elder (c. 350–c. 417), also previously a desert dweller, established a community in Jerusalem with Jerome's friend Rufinus of Aquileia.[7]

In fact, monasticism's earliest and largest growth was in the Eastern part of the Roman Empire. Some of the oldest monasteries still in existence today are located there, including Mount Athos in Greece and the Monastery of Saint Anthony in Egypt. Mission movements spread as far afield as the Arabian Peninsula, Central Asia, China, and India. But the trend later transformed the West. Martin of Tours (316–397) is often given the title "first monk in the West" due to his zeal in spreading the monastic life in Gaul (modern-day France).[8] Traditionally, he is said to have served in the Roman army, during which time he became a Christian. In the story he is most famous for, he gave half his cloak to a starving beggar "only to receive a vision that night in which Christ himself appeared clothed in the severed garment."[9] He soon left the army, saying "I am Christ's soldier; I am not allowed to fight."[10]

Martin became a missionary and a hermit, but disciples soon gathered around him—as they had done around so many Eastern desert fathers—and he gave them guidance. Eventually, he became bishop of Tours, but as bishop he still attempted to live as a monk and to found communities in his diocese. John Cassian (c. 360–435) traveled in Egypt and wrote the *Institutes* and the *Conferences of the Desert Fathers* around 420 (they were essentially "how they do it in Egypt" manuals) for Bishop Castor of Aptia Julia in Gaul. Both books would influence Benedict. Another circle of Western monasticism grew around Lérins on the French Riviera; its most famous monk was probably Vincent of Lérins (d. c. 445), who produced an enduring definition of the orthodox catholic faith: it is "that faith which has been believed everywhere, always, by all."[11]

Monasticism was not only growing in Gaul. When we think of Augustine (354–430) in North Africa, we may think first of the *Confessions* and its beautiful story of a conversion, or of the *City of God* and the way it influenced Western thought. But Augustine lived in a monastery before he became bishop, tried to turn his own bishop's household into a "quasi-monastery," and wrote a monastic rule of life, as well as commenting on what constituted the proper monastic life at many places in his writings.[12] Augustine gave as much space to the relationship of monks to each other as to their relationship to God, and the influence of his rule spread throughout both Gaul and Italy. One commentator has suggested that "with the Rule of Augustine western monasticism entered upon the road which led to Benedict."[13]

THE LIFE OF BENEDICT

Fifty years after Augustine died, Benedict was born in Nursia in northern Italy to lesser Roman nobility.[14] Much of what we know of him today comes from Pope Gregory the Great (c. 540–604), who wrote an outline of Benedict's life as part of his *Dialogues* about fifty years after Benedict had died. While the *Rule* never names its author, Gregory tells us that Benedict "wrote a rule for his monks, both excellent for discretion and also eloquent for its style."[15] Gregory never met Benedict but tells us that he got his information from "the relation of four of his disciples; namely, Constantinus, a most rare and reverent man, who was next Abbot after him; Valentinianus, who for many years had the charge of the Lateran Abbey; Simplicius, who was the third superior of his order; and lastly of Honoratus, who is now Abbot of that monastery in which he first began his holy life."[16] According to Gregory, Benedict had a twin sister, Scholastica, "dedicated from her infancy to our Lord"; she is considered the founder of Benedictine monasticism for women and was abbess of a convent at Plumbariola.[17]

Fifth-century Italy, notes one of Benedict's biographers, "was not . . . an auspicious place to be born. Benedict's home was a war-torn, disease-and-hunger-plagued land."[18] The defeat of Romulus Augustus by Germanic chief Odoacer in 476 had officially ended what was left of the Western Roman Empire and launched years of fighting, which ended with the Goth Theodoric the Great ruling in Italy in 493. His reign brought a time of peace, but fighting renewed on his death in 526 until, at last, Eastern emperor Justinian claimed jurisdiction over Italy as well in 554.

Like most young Roman nobles of years past, Benedict went (with his family) to study in Rome itself. There, he made the opposite choice of Augustine in Carthage when confronted with the "dull cycle of studying and drunken partying" of his fellow students; he chose to renounce everything for the life of a monk.[19] Around 500, he took his elderly nurse and left Rome for Enfide, where according to Gregory he wrought his first miracle—fixing a sieve that his nurse had accidentally broken. Disturbed by the fame the miracle brought him, he left her in Enfide and set out for Subaico.

At Subaico Benedict lived in a cave for three years, assisted by neighbors and eventually surrounded by disciples. He left his hermitage around 506 to serve as abbot of some monks in nearby Vicovaro.[20] The experiment ended badly—in fact, the monks tried to poison him—and he returned to the cave.

But Benedict was soon surrounded by so many followers that he ended up building thirteen monasteries, plus schools, in the area. He ruled as abbot over one of the monasteries and had deputies at the others. Around 530, after a conflict with a monk named Florentius, he left Subaico for Monte Cassino and built one large monastery there on the site of a former pagan temple to Apollo. Eventually, he established a foundation for another monastery at Terracina. At Monte Cassino, as far as we know, he finally wrote down a complete rule for his monks:

> To you, therefore, my words are now addressed,
> whoever you may be,
> who are renouncing your own will
> to do battle under the Lord Christ, the true King,
> and are taking up the strong, bright weapons of obedience.[21]

A School for the Lord's Service

Monasteries of the era were used to using what they liked from the many monastic rules available, and Benedict's eventual *Rule* drew on many sources, especially Cassian, Augustine, and a sixth-century manual known only as *The Rule of the Master*. The *Rule of the Master* shares a great deal of text with Benedict's production, and modern scholars think he used it as a basis for his own work. Divided into four sections, it first discusses the rule of the abbot and the spirituality of monks, then spends some time on prayer, then talks about life together, and finally "revisits the basic theology of monastic life with a particular emphasis on love."[22]

The *Rule* is both deeply theological and deeply practical. It speaks of the qualities needed for monastic life and advises monks on how to become closer to God through the "tools" or "instruments" of good works: "in the first place, to love the Lord God with the whole heart, the whole soul, the whole strength," as well as by observing scriptural precepts and ascetic practices.[23] Even today, Benedictines vow "stability, fidelity to the monastic way of life, and obedience" when they complete their novitiate and join the monastery.[24]

But the *Rule* also explains the nitty-gritty specifics of running a monastery. It instructs readers on how monks should organize their day, how they should read the Bible and other sacred texts, when they should nap, what they should wear, how they should hold goods in common, and how they should care for guests. In doing the last, it launched a long tradition of Benedictine hospitality: "Let all guests who arrive be received like Christ, / for He is going to say, / 'I came as a guest, and you received Me.'"[25] Benedict even addressed whether monks should drink alcohol:

> We read,
> it is true,
> that wine is by no means a drink for monastics;
> but since the monastics of our day cannot be persuaded
>   of this
> let us at least agree to drink sparingly and not to satiety,
> because "wine makes even the wise fall away."[26]

Women as well as men practiced this rule from the beginning—tradition tells us that they began doing so under the supervision of Scholastica. Although "attempts were made for a stricter enclosure [keeping nuns isolated from the outside world]," one historian notes that "the life of nuns was fundamentally the same as that of monks" and produced luminaries such as abbesses Hilda of Whitby (c. 614–680) and Hildegard of Bingen (1098–1179).[27]

The traditional date of Benedict's death is considered to be March 21, 547, shortly after his sister died on February 10. The monks laid him to rest, Gregory tells us, "in the Chapel of St. John the Baptist, which he had built to replace the altar of Apollo."[28] About thirty years after Benedict's death, the Lombards invaded Italy in 568, and the monastery at Monte Cassino was destroyed. Church tradition says that the monks took refuge in Rome along with the *Rule*. But it was still one of many rules. It only gradually became the norm for all of Western monasticism.

THE SPREAD OF THE *RULE*

We can first trace the spread of Benedictine monasticism to England, where Gregory sent missionaries in 596, and where the first monastery built was at Canterbury; one Benedictine has called Canterbury "the cradle, not only of English monasticism, but also of English Christian culture."[29] Included among English Benedictine monks whose influence would reach down the ages was church historian and scholar the Venerable Bede (c. 672–735), author of *An Ecclesiastical History of the English People*, and much later Anselm of Canterbury (1033–1109). Anselm was an abbot, archbishop, and one of the Middle Ages' greatest theologians; his *Cur Deus Homo* ("Why God Became Man"), written between 1094 and 1098, is one of the church's classic statements on how Christ redeems us.[30]

Meanwhile, in the early seventh century Benedictines reached into France, spread into Germanic territories, and rose again in Italy at Bobbio. Monasticism of a Celtic type had spread already into some of these areas through the evangelistic efforts of Irish missionary Columban (d. 615), but Benedict's *Rule* began to displace Columban's. In 720, the monastery at Monte Cassino was reopened, soon a central "symbol to be admired, and to be consulted for interpretation of the rule and tradition."[31]

Despite this slow spread, the West was "far from being totally Benedictine by the year 800."[32] What really helped the process along were Charlemagne (742–814) and his descendants. King of the Franks, a Germanic tribe, from the 740s, he claimed the throne of the Holy Roman Empire from the year 800 on (more on him in the next chapter). Charlemagne not only revived the title of the Roman emperors but attempted to standardize the practices of the church throughout his realm through a set of rules he called *correctio*, putting things back into order. "Local towns competed with each other to show their assent to its requirements," as one historian put it.[33] This standardization included monasteries, which he preferred should be run under the "Roman rule" of Benedict.[34]

Another Benedict, Benedict of Aniane (c. 750–821), took this desire and ran with it. This second Benedict had spent time at the Carolingian court but later became a monk and founded a monastery near the Pyrenees in modern France. His monastery grew to over three hundred monks and soon adopted the *Rule*, and it drew the attention of Charlemagne's son and eventual successor, Louis the Pious (778–840).

Louis put Benedict of Aniane in charge of standardizing monastic governance in France and Germany, based on the rules at use in the monastery built under Louis's protection at Inde. The second Benedict established a system of official visitors from Inde to other monasteries and called a synod in 817 to help coordinate and standardize efforts. He also collected examples of other rules in use and wrote a commentary on the first Benedict's *Rule*.

Monasteries of this renewed Holy Roman Empire in the West became wealthy and politically powerful. They were centers of scholarship and missionary activity, but they also fit comfortably into the feudal governments of their lands, with a secular lord to whom they owed obedience—and who usually appointed their abbot—and serfs to farm their land and do much of the work that Benedict of Nursia had pictured the monks doing for themselves. "The camel's nose," as one writer puts it, "was already under the tent-flap."[35]

A rhythm was set in place, like the swinging of a pendulum; Western monasticism would thrive and become connected inextricably to the flow of the world around it, and then some reform movement would arise attempting to bring people back to the purity of Benedict of Nursia's original vision. Against this swinging of the pendulum, the calls for reform that would echo from Martin Luther and others seven centuries later (discussed further in chap. 5) come into sharper focus. Reforms were needed, but Luther was not the first to have said so.

CLUNY AND THE CISTERCIANS

After Louis died, the Carolingian empire began to disintegrate, and western Europe was plagued by war and corruption. While some individual monasteries thrived, it was almost a hundred years before the pendulum swung again with the founding of a monastery at Cluny, in Burgundy, in 910. This monastery was unusual because its founder, Duke William of Aquitaine, gave up the right that was his as the founder to continue appointing an abbot. (The appointing of abbots by secular lords was one of the struggles monks faced in maintaining the discipline Benedict had envisioned.) After placing Berno (c. 850–927) over Cluny, Duke William allowed the monks to elect an abbot of their choosing from then on. Berno, who already ruled two other monasteries, established the *Rule* in all three.

For over two hundred years, Cluny and its fellow monasteries Baume and Gigny were ruled by "a series of abbots whose sanctity was equal to their discretion and administrative ability."[36] Among them were Odo (c. 878–942) and Hugh (1024–1109). Cluny itself soon had many monasteries dependent on it at various administrative levels, and even among nondependent monasteries the practice of the *Rule* at Cluny, called its "usages," spread all over western Europe from England to Italy.

Cluny and the monasteries influenced by it maintained the high level of scholarship that Benedictines by now were famous for.[37] They also focused closely on the observance of prayer and worship. While manual labor was no longer required (*conversi*, laymen under the rule of the monastery, now did this), the monks spent long hours in prayer and were enjoined to keep silence at all times otherwise, speaking only in sign language.

But again, growth was a mixed blessing. More and more monks were ordained to the priesthood, in part to help supply the large numbers of liturgies that were constantly kept going. (Benedict had not been ordained and had not foreseen large numbers of monks also being priests.) Monasteries lived off the proceeds from their estates, farmed by the *conversi* and by serfs, rather than working the land themselves. The *commendam* system, whereby an outsider was appointed abbot, continued to grow. The wealth and power of many abbots, even those who were still monks elected by other monks, made them "lords and prelates" of the "nobility of the country," living in palaces outside the monastery walls and "enjoying the rights and insignia of bishops."[38] There were more monasteries than there were people with vocations to be monks and nuns. Financial, liturgical, and spiritual decadence reigned.

Against this background, a group of monks forming a new monastery at Molesme in Burgundy in the late eleventh century argued for returning to the simplicity of Benedict's "school for the service of the Lord." Opposed by their fellows, they left Molesme and established a monastery at Cîteaux in 1098; the Latin name of the town, Cisterce, gave them the name by which they are known today—Cistercians.[39]

At Cîteaux and elsewhere, the Cistercians established their monasteries in solitude: "No business was to be conducted in the neighborhood of the monastery, no nobleman was to be buried in the monastery church."[40] They enforced strict poverty, manual labor for everyone, and simplicity in worship. This new approach to Benedictine practice was attractive to many. In fact, it was so attractive that eventually in 1145 a Cistercian, Bernardo da Pisa, was elected pope as Eugene III—not quite the complete separation from the world envisioned at Cîteaux.

OTHER OPTIONS

Benedict's was never the only medieval Western rule. In the late eleventh century, Bruno of Cologne (c. 1030–1101), a disciple of one of the original Cistercians, founded the Carthusians, named for their founding abbey in Chartreuse in the French Alps; he gave them a rule of his own devising. Sometime in the twelfth century the Carmelites also arose (so called because they claim to have originated from a group of hermits who had gathered on Mount Carmel), focused on both contemplation and service. In the early thirteenth century they asked the Western patriarch of Jerusalem, Alberto Avogadro, for a rule of life—still followed by Carmelites today—and the order was approved by the pope in 1226. They migrated west in the 1230s and 1240s when tensions increased between West and East. The proclamation of the Crusades, about which you will hear more in chapter four, produced the growth of "fighting" orders.[41]

Around the end of the twelfth century, a completely new kind of religious life came into being: the so-called mendicant (begging) orders.[42] Perhaps, people thought, the problems of corruption that arose when monasteries owned property would not be so prevalent if they did not. Francis of Assisi (c. 1181–1226), a rich young Italian nobleman who was tiring of his life of pleasure, went on a pilgrimage to Rome. Upon returning, he had a vision in a chapel at San Damiano, where he saw Christ telling him (so the story goes), "Francis, Francis, go and repair My house which, as you can see, is falling into ruins."

Francis began preaching and soon gathered around him groups of "friars" (from the Latin word for brother, *frater*), who took vows of poverty and spent their days as traveling preachers depending on the support of their audiences. They were given papal approval in 1209 as a mendicant order.[43] Francis's friend Clare of Assisi (1194–1253) founded a Franciscan order for women, the Poor Clares, although they remained enclosed and did not beg. Dominic de Guzmán (c. 1170–1221) founded the Dominicans in 1216 as a mendicant order specifically devoted to preaching; they adopted the Rule of Saint Augustine to govern themselves. The Dominicans were known for scholarship as well as preaching, and they would nurture one of the Middle Ages' most famous scholars, Thomas Aquinas (c. 1225–1274).

Aquinas's family wanted him to become a Benedictine: it was a suitable career for the younger sons of Sicilian nobles, and they in fact lived not far from Monte Cassino. But at nineteen, the young man was drawn to become a mendicant preacher and apologist instead. His family was furious, especially his mother: "Her youngest child was destined to be the abbot of St. Benedict's monastery, not a beggar in an order despised by clergy and traditional monks alike."[44] After a year of drama, his family finally allowed him to escape out the bedroom window to maintain their good name, and to join the Dominicans. Aquinas was one of the chief builders of scholastic theology, which would dominate Western Christendom for seven hundred years, in his *Summa Theologiae* and other works. He was eventually canonized in the fourteenth century and named a doctor of the church in the sixteenth.

People had also been following the Rule of Saint Augustine throughout the Middle Ages—mainly groups of clergy called canons around certain large churches, although prominent women like canoness and mystic Hrotsvitha of Gandersheim (c. 935–c. 1001) were also Augustinians.[45] This kind of life became more popular in the thirteenth century, as did the use of the Rule of Saint Augustine by groups of lay hermits. This movement formally became the Augustinian Order in the 1250s, with a special focus on study, pastoral care (many Augustinians were priests), and mission.

Finally, many lay people who could not or did not want to join a religious order still desired to commit themselves to a deeper Christian life.[46] Some joined "third orders" sponsored by the Franciscans and Dominicans, groups that lived in the world while following a version of the monastic rule. Others became Beguines (women) and Beghards (men); famous thirteenth-century mystic Mechthild of Magdeburg (c. 1207–c. 1282) was a Beguine. Still others became part of the Brethren of the Common Life, a group that grew out of the Modern Devotion movement in Germany, and also the group for whom Thomas à Kempis (c. 1380–1471) penned his classic *The Imitation of Christ*.

Most of these groups were semimonastic communities whose members pooled their property and spent much time in prayer and devotion but did not take vows and were free to leave at any time.[47] Some who desired a deeper life undertook a more solitary path inspired by monastic traditions of hermitage, such as Julian of Norwich (1341–c. 1416), one of many who enclosed themselves in small cells attached to churches. Called anchorites, Julian and others like her spent time in prayer and contemplation; through a window in each cell they dispensed spiritual counsel and received the Eucharist (as well as deliveries of food).[48]

So, that troubled Augustinian friar who would spark a sixteenth-century conflagration, Martin Luther, was not alone in seeking a better way. He sought an end to corruption throughout the church, to be sure, but many of the issues that he put his reforming finger on centered on both the promise and the problems with the monastic ideal:

> The promise of a truly Christian society, in which people lived out their baptismal vocation in the station to which God had called them, seemed elusive. The tension between

the ascetic demands of mainstream medieval piety and the joys and demands of life in this world seemed irrecon-cilable. Ironically, this resulted from medieval Christian-ity's success as well as its failure. Over time a critical mass of lay Christians had come to take the summons to live out their baptismal calling in the world with deadly seriousness. That was why Martin Luther's radical solutions soon gained so much traction—solutions that created tensions and paradoxes of their own.[49]

MODERN MONKS

Monasticism did not end with the Reformation, of course. The sixteenth century saw the birth of quite a few orders that at-tempted to recapture the original purity and passion of the movement, the most famous of which were the Jesuits. The Council of Trent, Catholicism's reforming council from 1545 to 1563, took up monastic issues along with its other decrees at-tempting to reorganize and renew the church. The decree they issued, "Concerning Regulars and Nuns," was straightforward in its expectation: "All Regulars [i.e., monks] shall order their lives in accordance with what is prescribed by the rule which they have professed."[50] Trent addressed perennial problems: the wealth of monasteries, the failure of abbots to have the care of only one monastery and live there themselves, and the tendency to make young women enter convents at early ages.

Through the intervening centuries, Benedict's original ideal has continued to draw those troubled by the problems of the world—and the church. All the permutations of Benedictines, as well as the Dominicans, Franciscans, Augustinians, Carthu-sians, Carmelites, Jesuits, and many other smaller groups, remain in existence today as Roman Catholic religious orders. New ones have arisen, too: New Melleray, on whose grounds I walked, is a Trappist abbey, heir to a seventeenth-century reform of the Cistercians.

In the mid-nineteenth century, Anglicans in England and the United States became the first Protestants to revive the practice of monasticism, and today you can find Anglican Benedictines as well as those who follow other rules.[51] Reformed Protestant pastor Roger Schütz (1915–2005), more commonly known as Brother Roger, founded Taizé in the 1950s in France as an ecumenical religious order accepting both Catholics and Protestants. In the late twentieth century a movement called the "new monasticism," associated with names like Shane Claiborne (b. 1975) and Jonathan Wilson-Hartgrove (b. 1981), launched among a loosely connected network of broadly evangelical Protestant thinkers and communities, preaching a message of solidarity with the poor and life in community.[52] And thousands who would never call themselves monastic or say they lived by a rule of life have warmed to the message of bestsellers like Thomas Merton's *The Seven Storey Mountain,* Kathleen Norris's *The Cloister Walk,* Dallas Willard's *The Spirit of the Disciplines,* Richard Foster's *Celebration of Discipline,* and Rod Dreher's *The Benedict Option.*[53]

Though modern monastic movements are diverse, their messages and their rules of life are surprisingly similar—*and* surprisingly similar to Benedict's original vision. Pray. Live simply. Practice hospitality. Worship. Receive Communion. Treat others with the love of Christ. Be accountable to each other in the Christian community. "But Christians can, and should, do these things without a rule," some may protest. True. Yet Benedict was wise in knowing that our love for God flows strongest when it flows in defined channels, that service to others grows best out of our gratitude for God's great mercy, and that we learn much in a school for the service of the Lord. His vision has sometimes been corrupted. It has frequently been imitated. But it has never been surpassed.

RECOMMENDED READING

Benedict, Saint. *RB 1980: The Rule of St. Benedict in Latin and English with Notes*. Translated and edited by Timothy Fry. Collegeville, MN: Liturgical Press, 1981.

Bredero, Adriaan. *Christendom and Christianity in the Middle Ages*. Translated by Reinder Bruinsma. Grand Rapids, MI: Eerdmans, 1994.

Butcher, Carmen Acevedo. *Man of Blessing: A Life of St. Benedict*. Brewster, MA: Paraclete Press, 2006.

Chittister, Joan. *The Radical Christian Life: A Year with Saint Benedict*. Collegeville, MN: Liturgical Press, 2011.

Evans, G. R. *The I. B. Tauris History of Monasticism: The Western Tradition*. London: Tauris, 2016.

Norris, Kathleen. *The Cloister Walk*. New York: Riverhead, 1996.

four

THE EXCOMMUNICATION OF PATRIARCH KERULARIOS BY POPE LEO IX VIA CARDINAL HUMBERT (1054)

"We have sensed here both a great good, whence we greatly rejoice in the Lord, and the greatest evil, whence we lament in misery."

It was July 16, 1054; the great church of Hagia Sophia (Holy Wisdom) in the city founded by Constantine, Constantinople, was prepared for a service of the Divine Liturgy (Eucharist). Three legates from the pope in Rome—including his secretary, Cardinal Humbert of Silva Candida—made their way into the church, but not to worship:

> They placed a sealed papal document called a "bull" on the altar and marched out. The bull proclaimed the patriarch of Constantinople and his associates excommunicated, no longer in communion with the church, no longer allowed to receive the grace of God through the sacraments. When the cardinal passed through the western door, he shook the dust from his feet and said, "Let God look and judge." A deacon,

guessing the contents of the bull, ran after Humbert in great distress and begged him to take it back. Humbert refused, and the deacon dropped the document in the street.[1]

The picture here is just as dramatic as the one—more famous to Westerners—of Martin Luther nailing to the cathedral door the protest that split Western Christendom. And just as the actual story of the beginning of the Protestant Reformation is far more complex than can be expressed in that single moment, so too what came to be known as the Great Schism between Eastern and Western Christendom is far more complex than what happened at the altar of Hagia Sophia. The mutual excommunications issued in 1054—the one proclaimed here, and the one that Kerularios issued to the legates as a result of this event— were only one step on a long journey taking East and West ever farther apart.

HE IS RISEN INDEED

Some years ago, my husband and I visited a modern-day Antiochian Orthodox Church, Saint Stephen the Protomartyr in South Plainfield, New Jersey, for their Easter vigil service, the Great and Holy Feast of Pascha.[2] Orthodox Christians celebrate Easter on a different date from Western Christians because the Eastern church still uses a form of the Julian calendar to determine its date, so our celebrations of Easter in our Anglican setting were already over.[3]

This vigil (which some Protestants and Roman Catholics celebrate today as well) begins at darkness on the night of Holy Saturday, contains many Scripture readings telling the story of God's saving acts, and concludes with a joyous celebration of Communion. The heart of the service, after the reading of Scripture and before the holy meal, is the proclamation of

Christ's resurrection with the words "Christ is risen from the dead, trampling down death by death, and to those in the tombs bestowing life!" It is customary for the congregation then to greet each other with the words "Christ is risen! He is risen indeed!"

The liturgy was conducted mainly in English, but we were encouraged to greet each other in our own languages, and as those around us reminded us that Christ was risen, we heard these words in Romanian, Arabic, and Syriac—the last being the closest language today to the Aramaic Jesus would have spoken. This was a new world to me as a Western Christian. How had I become so disconnected from it? To understand, it is necessary to step back centuries to our old friend Constantine.

When Constantine assumed the throne as sole emperor, culture in the West centered on Rome (though Diocletian had moved the administrative capital to Mediolanum in 286). The city of Byzantium, in modern-day Turkey, became Constantine's newly renamed capital in the East. Several generations after Constantine's death, Germanic tribes from northern Europe— the Romans called them "barbarians" from the Greek word *bárbaros*, "babbler"—began to move into the western half of the empire. In 410, one of these tribes, the Visigoths, sacked Rome as part of a larger invasion of Italy, and in 476 Odoacer, a Germanic chieftain, deposed the emperor in the West, Romulus Augustus, and took the title King of Italy. He declared himself a client of the emperor in the East, Zeno.[4]

Then, in the early 600s, a new religion arose in the area we now call the Middle East—Islam, based on the teachings of Muhammad (c. 570–632) and increasingly spread by armies of the caliphs (Muslim rulers). With Islam conquering territories around the Mediterranean, contact between the remains of the Western empire and the still-flourishing Eastern branch became even more difficult. The church in the West began to look north and not east for assistance, and the popes became closer to the Franks, who had by this point conquered large portions of western Europe. Culture and language began to drift apart:

> The days when educated men were bilingual were over. By the year 450, there were few in the West who could read Greek, and after 600, although Byzantium still called itself the *Roman* Empire, it was rare for a Byzantine to speak Latin, the language of the Romans. . . . They no longer drew upon the same sources nor read the same books.[5]

Church administration differed, too. Rome, Constantinople, Alexandria, Antioch, and Jerusalem had historically been considered the five great sees, or seats of bishops, in the church, each with a claim to foundation by an apostle. Four were in the Eastern empire; only Rome was in the West: "In the East there was a strong sense of the quality of all bishops, of the collegial and conciliar nature of the Church. The East acknowledged the Pope as the first bishop in the church, but saw him as the first among equals."[6]

There was also a series of strong emperors in the East who served as a counterbalance to the patriarchs (as the Eastern bishops in the apostolic sees were called). In the West, though, the pope was the only bishop in an apostolic see, and a source of stability in a constantly shifting political landscape. He came to be seen as the ultimate authority on both sacred and secular matters.[7] The East, meanwhile,

> didn't care if the Western Church was centralized, as long as the papacy did not interfere in the East. . . . The pope increasingly issued commands not only to ecclesiastical subordinates but to secular rulers as well. Still, the Eastern church didn't mind—as long as the pope claimed absolute power only in the West.[8]

Icons and a Golden Tongue

These political, administrative, cultural, and language separa-
tions all went hand in hand with theological distinctions as East
and West grew further apart:

> Byzantium was a civilization of great wealth and learning,
> and many educated laymen took an active interest in the-
> ology.... Latin thought was influenced by Roman law,
> while Greeks understood theology in the context of worship.
> Regarding the Crucifixion, Latins thought primarily of
> Christ the victim on the Cross, Greeks of Christ the victor
> over death. Latins talked more about redeeming sinners,
> Greeks, about the deification of humanity. There were also
> a few practical differences: the Greeks allowed married
> clergy; the Latins insisted on priestly celibacy. The two sides
> had different rules about fasting. The Greeks used leavened
> bread in the Eucharist, the Latins unleavened bread.[9]

The story of Constantine and Nicaea from our first two
chapters, not to mention the beginnings of monasticism in the
previous chapter, is mostly an Eastern story.[10] Mighty theologians like Ambrose (c. 340–397) and Augustine and philosophers like Boethius (c. 477–524) certainly arose in the West after
Nicaea. But Greek fathers like Athanasius, Cyril of Alexandria,
and the Cappadocians—Basil of Caesarea; his brother Gregory
of Nyssa (c. 335–c. 395); and their friend and eventual patriarch
of Constantinople, Gregory of Nazianzus (329–389)—all con-
tributed crucially to the development and maintenance of orthodox Christian doctrine.

At around the same time as these "three wise men from the
east," John Chrysostom from Antioch (c. 347–c. 407) grew
famous as an "eloquent and uncompromising" preacher; his
nickname *chrysostomos* means "golden mouth."[11] One of his

most famous sermons is still read at every Eastern Orthodox service of Pascha. It concludes:

> Christ is risen, and the demons are fallen. Christ is risen, and the angels rejoice. Christ is risen, and life reigns. Christ is risen, and not one dead remains in the grave. For Christ, being risen from the dead, is become the first fruits of those who have fallen asleep. To Him be glory and dominion unto ages of ages. Amen.[12]

The Greek church also became known for the beauty and mysticism of its worship—dominated above all by the presence of icons, widespread by the sixth century. These were images of Christ, Mary, and the saints; they covered almost every available space in the sanctuary, were composed not as art but as an expression of prayer, were "large, bold, formal, lacking any sentimentality," and were intended to convey that worshipers stood "in the presence of the living God, together with the saints and the righteous of every age."[13] Believers commonly venerated them by kissing them, bowing, or prostrating themselves on the floor in front of them.

A large screen, called the *iconostasis*, separated the congregational area from the altar; much of the service was conducted behind this. Nearly everything was sung. There were no pews. Candles were everywhere. The language of the liturgy was "elaborate, flowery, and highly poetic."[14] Such worship did not differ as much from Western Christian worship as it does today—in the medieval Catholic West, there were no pews either, and people often did their private devotions while the Eucharist was going on—but the music and the words of the liturgy and the imagery of the icons were unmistakably Greek.

One of the greatest conflicts in the East centered on the use of these icons. In the early eighth century, Emperor Leo III was convinced by arguments from Exodus 20:4 that icons, especially when venerated, were the kinds of graven images forbidden by the Scriptures.[15] Around 730 he had his soldiers destroy a large icon at the palace gate, causing riots.

Leo's son, Constantine V, continued the campaign against icons, in 754 calling a council, which he called the Seventh Ecumenical Council and which forbade their use. Following the council "thousands were exiled, tortured, or martyred" because of their desire to use icons over the next thirty years.[16] One of Orthodoxy's greatest medieval theologians, John of Damascus (c. 675–749), argued for the use of icons in his *First Apology* and differentiated their veneration from the worship due to God alone:

> In former times, God, who is without form or body, could never be depicted. But now when God is seen in the flesh conversing with men (*Baruch* 3:38), I make an image of the God whom I see. I do not worship matter; I worship the Creator of matter who became matter for my sake.[17]

Finally, in 787 Empress Irene of Athens, who supported the use of icons, called another council. Held at Nicaea and recognized by both East and West today as the rightful Seventh Ecumenical Council, it depended greatly on the writings of John of Damascus in determining "that icons, though they may not be worshipped, may be honored."[18] After another brief period of protest from 815 to 843, icons were permanently restored by Empress Theodora.[19]

CHARLEMAGNE, PHOTIUS, AND THE NICENE CREED

Without active conflict between them, East and West might have continued pursuing their complementary approaches to the faith of the Nicene Creed, culturally adapted but still unified. Unfortunately, active conflict came.

On Christmas Day 800, Pope Leo III crowned the King of the Franks, Charles the Great (the Latin form of his name and title being *Charlemagne*), as Holy Roman Emperor at Saint Peter's Basilica in Rome. Charlemagne affected to have been surprised, but he had actually presided over a council earlier that month that voted to make him emperor. When he had been crowned, a chronicle noted,

> All the faithful Romans, seeing how he loved the holy Roman church and its vicar and how he defended them, cried out with one voice by the will of God and of St. Peter, the key-bearer of the kingdom of heaven, "To Charles, most pious Augustus, crowned by God, great and peace-loving emperor, life and victory." This was said three times before the sacred tomb of blessed Peter the apostle, with the invocation of many saints. And so he was instituted by all as emperor of the Romans.[20]

There was, of course, a problem with this: there was already an augustus ruling the Romans in the East—at this point it was Empress Irene, the first female ruler.[21] Some Western leaders argued that the throne was actually vacant since a woman now occupied it, but Charlemagne pronounced himself obedient to the East and sought recognition from Byzantium. Such recognition was not forthcoming: the Byzantine court "regarded Charlemagne as an intruder and the papal coronation as an act of schism."[22] Eventually Byzantine emperor Michael I recognized Charlemagne as *an* emperor in 812 but not as *the* emperor.

A little more than fifty years later, conflict again arose. The patriarch of Constantinople, Ignatius, resigned under personal pressure from Emperor Michael III and was replaced by lay theologian Photius. Photius followed normal procedure in

sending a letter to Pope Nicholas I to announce that he had succeeded to the office: "Normally, the pope would immediately
recognize a new patriarch. But Nicholas balked."[23] Nicholas was
"a reforming pope, with an exalted idea—at least according to the
Orthodox—of the prerogatives of his office."[24] He decided Ignatius had been wrongly treated and that he should look into the
matter, and in 861 he sent legates who were courteously received
by Photius and presided at a council in Constantinople that declared Photius to be legitimate.

But when the legates returned, Nicholas held *another* council
at Rome in 863 and declared Ignatius legitimate and Photius
deposed. Photius ignored Nicholas. But along with the political
issues, theological and practical ones were fermenting.

To understand the theological issue at stake, we need to return
to the Nicene Creed. As modified at Constantinople, its third
section contained the phrase that the Holy Spirit is "the Lord
and Giver of life, who proceeds from the Father [in Latin, *qui ex
Patre procedit*], who with the Father and the Son together is
worshiped and together glorified." But in the sixth century, some
Christians in Spain—eager to counteract still-active Arianism—
began to say instead that the Spirit "proceeds from the Father
and the Son" (*qui ex Patre Filioque procedit*).[25]

At the third Council of Toledo in 589, a local Spanish council,
the churches in Spain officially adopted this new version of the
creed. The practice made its way to the Franks, where Charlemagne's churches officially adopted it in 794 at the local Council
of Frankfurt. More than that, they accused the Byzantine church
of "heresy because they recited the Creed in its original form."[26]
Pope Leo, for all that he was ready to crown a Holy Roman Emperor, was not ready to change the creed, and said so in 808.

When Orthodox theologians heard of the practice, they were
"sharply critical"; they had theological objections to the way the

new phrase described the Trinity, and, even more strongly, they argued that

> the Ecumenical Councils specifically forbade any change to be introduced into the Creed; and if an addition has to be made, certainly nothing short of another Ecumenical Council is competent to make it. The Creed is the common possession of the whole Church.[27]

Meanwhile West and East, in sending out missionaries, had met in Bulgaria. There the khan (ruler) of Bulgaria, Boris, wavered back and forth between the two, finally accepting baptism from the Byzantines in 865. But when his church was not given as much independence as he liked, he switched back to favoring the Western missionaries, who immediately began attacking Eastern practices such as married clergy and the refusal to use the *filioque* clause, as it is known.

Pope Nicholas supported the use of the *filioque* in Bulgaria. Photius opposed it. He wrote to the patriarchs of Jerusalem, Antioch, and Alexandria accusing Pope Nicholas of heresy— and then, for good measure, called a council at Constantinople that called Nicholas "a heretic who ravages the vineyard of the Lord."[28]

Further trouble might have followed except that unrelated political intrigue at court in 867 resulted in the assassination of Michael III—the emperor who had started the whole issue by exiling Ignatius. Michael's murderer succeeded him and gave the patriarchate back to Ignatius, and Pope Nicholas died that same year. A local council in 869 condemned Photius and claimed Bulgaria for the East; Boris agreed and switched sides again. Eventually, Ignatius and Photius reconciled, Photius succeeded Ignatius when he died, and a final council in 879 reversed all the earlier condemnations. For the time being.

HERE WE GO AGAIN

For a little over a hundred years, there were no major conflicts, though in the West there was a steady centralization of papal power. Then in the early decades of the eleventh century, several things happened. First, in 1009, when Pope Sergius IV assumed the papacy, he sent a letter to the patriarch of Constantinople (also called Sergius) that included the *filioque*. Possibly as a result, Sergius the patriarch did not record the new pope's name on the Diptychs, "lists, kept by each Patriarch, of the other patriarchs, living and departed, whom he recognizes as orthodox."[29] But these lists had not always been kept diligently before. However, in 1014, Henry II was crowned as Holy Roman Emperor in Rome in a service that included the singing of the *filioque*; this added fuel to the fire.

Then trouble arose between Normans and Greeks in Italy in the 1050s. The western tribe of Normans, who were trying to conquer southern Italy, tried to make the Byzantine Greeks who lived there use Latin practices of worship and devotion. Patriarch Kerularios retaliated by closing Latin churches in Constantinople in 1052. However, he let Pope Leo IX know that he was amenable to discussing the matter, and Leo dispatched his legates.

Unfortunately, one was Cardinal Humbert: "Both he and [Kerularios] were men of stiff and intransigent temper, whose encounter was not likely to promote good will among Christians."[30] Humbert treated the patriarch rudely in their first encounter. The patriarch called off any further meetings. Humbert decided to excommunicate him.

The bull Humbert left on the altar, though proclaimed under papal authority, was actually largely written by Humbert. The sentence from it that begins this chapter, though beautiful and sad on its own, prefaces nasty accusations—mostly untrue—about Eastern worship practices. Humbert accused the East of rebaptizing, castrating candidates for ordination, and omitting the *filioque* (a particularly bizarre accusation, since Westerners had added it!). Even true statements about Eastern practice, such as the Easterners' use of leavened bread and married clergy, were expressed spitefully. Although Humbert did not know it at the time, Leo IX had died four months earlier, making the bull technically invalid. After leaving the bull, Humbert and the other legates went home to Italy. Kerularios promptly called a synod that excommunicated them.

Even so, it was thought at the time that "the misunderstandings could be cleared up without too much difficulty. The dispute remained something of which ordinary Christians in east and west were largely unaware."[31] After all, things had gotten pretty awful between Photius and Nicholas. Surely a way out could be found again.

CRUSADE FOR WHAT?

Despite the growing distrust—and the exertion by eleventh-century popes, like Gregory VII, of a strong and centralizing hand—about forty years later a way seemed to open.[32] Alexios I, the emperor in the East, sent envoys to the Council of Piacenza in 1095 and asked for the help of Pope Urban II. Islam had continued to grow, and Muslim forces had conquered portions of Alexios's territory. There was particular concern because they had conquered sites in the Holy Land. Could Urban perhaps send a few troops to help out?

Urban sent more than a few troops. He preached a Crusade, as the saying came to be known, sending forth the call at the Council of Clermont in November 1095. In a letter he wrote shortly afterwards, the same message is clear:

> A barbaric fury has deplorably afflicted and laid waste the
> churches of God in the regions of the Orient. More than

this, blasphemous to say, it has even grasped in intolerable servitude ... the Holy City of Christ, glorified by His passion and resurrection.[33]

Two groups in fact set out to fulfill the pope's and the emperor's wishes: the unofficial People's Crusade, a group of peasants led by priest and ascetic Peter the Hermit, and the official Prince's Crusade, an organized expedition of nobles. The peasants were quickly defeated, but the nobles recaptured Nicaea, Antioch, and Jerusalem by 1099.[34] They did not hand them back to the East and go home but set up Western settlements with Latin churches and established Latin patriarchs in the new Principality of Antioch and Kingdom of Jerusalem. There was at that point no Greek patriarch in Jerusalem, and there, at least for some time, the two groups worshiped together at the ancient holy places. But there was already a Greek patriarch in Antioch, and there "throne was set up against throne and altar against altar."[35]

Two more Crusades soon followed. (There would ultimately be nine.) Unlike the first, they were not very successful, and Muslims recaptured Jerusalem in 1187. There was now a Greek patriarch in Jerusalem, but the West continued to name Latin patriarchs, who resided at Acre: "Two rival bishops claimed the same throne and two hostile congregations existed in the same city."[36]

In 1202, Pope Innocent III preached a Fourth Crusade to recapture Jerusalem. Sadly, most of the Crusaders never got there. They were persuaded to detour to Constantinople by businessmen who were financing the venture and by Alexios, son of recently deposed Byzantine emperor Isaac II. Alexios hoped the Crusaders would help him and his father in the struggle to retake his father's throne, which they did; but his ascension as

Alexios IV with Isaac II as his co-emperor did not end the political infighting. Relations between Eastern citizens and the Western army camped in their city steadily grew worse and more violent.

Finally, the Westerners lost patience with both the politics and the population. To them, this world of icons and leavened bread, of gold-tinged mosaics and liturgical mysticism, of married priests with long beards and unintelligible Greek liturgy, seemed as alien as the Islamic practices they had originally set out to conquer. For three days, they sacked the city of Constantinople—destroying one of the greatest centers of culture and art the world had ever known:

> Eastern Christendom has never forgotten those three appalling days of pillage. "Even the Saracens [Muslims] are merciful and kind," protested Nicetas Choniates, "compared with these men who wear the Cross of Christ on their shoulders [a sign of a Crusader]." What shocked the Greeks more than anything was the wanton and systematic sacrilege of the Crusaders. How could men who had specially dedicated themselves to God's service treat the things of God in such a way? As the Byzantines watched the Crusaders tear to pieces the altar and icon screen in the church of the Holy Wisdom, and set prostitutes on the Patriarch's throne, they must have felt that those who did such things were not Christians in the same sense as themselves.[37]

A few Crusaders went on to Jerusalem. Most of them went home, singing a song that translates as "City of Constantinople, so long ungodly."[38]

Innocent III protested the results of the Crusade in a famous letter, writing shortly after the sack of the city:

How, indeed, is the Greek church to be brought back into ecclesiastical union and to a devotion for the Apostolic See when she has been beset with so many afflictions and persecutions that she sees in the Latins only an example of perdition and the works of darkness, so that she now, and with reason, detests the Latins more than dogs?[39]

But the letter did no actual good. The Byzantine Empire, already a shadow of its former self, was split into three parts; Crusaders established a "Latin Empire" in the area around Constantinople and put a Westerner, Baldwin of Flanders, on the throne. None of the remaining five Crusades ever recaptured Jerusalem. A famous historian remarked of the incident, "The Crusaders brought not peace but a sword; and the sword was to sever Christendom."[40]

The Byzantines took the throne back in 1261, and there were still various attempts made to reconcile East and West, including the Council of Lyons in 1274 and the Council of Florence in 1439, which produced a failed Bull of Union. One Greek noble responded to Florence, "I would rather see the Muslim turban in the midst of the city than the Latin miter."[41] Meanwhile, more and more of the weakened Eastern empire was captured by Muslim armies. In 1453, Constantinople fell to the Turkish army. They renamed the city Kostantiniyye and eventually Istanbul. Hagia Sophia, the church where the bull had been laid on the altar, was turned into a mosque, then a museum in 1935, and then a mosque again in 2020.

INTO ALL THE WORLD

This may have been the end of the Byzantine Empire, but it was not the end of the Orthodox Church. Its missionary activity, as we've already seen, had begun in earnest in the ninth century. The most famous Orthodox missionaries, Cyril (826–869) and

Methodius (815–885), carried the gospel to Moravia—an act that meant the translation of the Greek liturgy into the language of the Slavs. The resulting Old Church Slavonic is still used in the services of some Orthodox churches today.[42]

Their disciples and others spread Christianity to Bulgaria, Serbia, Romania, and Russia, where it took firm root. This was especially true in Russia, where ruler Vladimir the Great converted in 998, chronicles tell, after consulting with representatives of Islam, Judaism, and Western Christianity as well. He ultimately sent messengers to Hagia Sophia; these messengers experienced the Divine Liturgy and reported back, "We no longer knew whether we were in heaven or on earth." Orthodoxy became the state church in Russia for over a thousand years.

Each of these countries gained a patriarch of their own and services in their own language, and they became churches deeply wedded to state and culture—an issue with which modern-day Orthodoxy continues to wrestle: "They have sometimes tended to think of their faith as primarily Serb, Russian, or Bulgar, and to forget that it is primarily Orthodox and Catholic."[43] Of course, western Europe wrestled with the same problem, as the history of monasticism has shown us abundantly. It was part of the complicated legacy Constantine had bequeathed his adopted faith.

Today, there are sixteen main *autocephalous* (self-governing) Orthodox churches, and many other autonomous national churches under the supervision of the patriarch of Constantinople—each with its own culture and frequently worshiping in its own language. When Orthodox immigrants came to North America, they brought their churches, and you can find Greek, Romanian, Syrian, and many other ethnic churches in the United States today, as well as the Orthodox Church in America, which has its roots in Russian missions in Alaska and became independent after the Russian Revolution of 1917.[44]

In 1964, a meeting of Pope Paul VI and Greek patriarch Athenagoras led to a mutual withdrawal of the excommunications of 1054. The document they produced in 1965 was proclaimed simultaneously at the Second Vatican Council—about which we will have much more to say in the final chapter—and at a ceremony in Istanbul, formerly Constantinople.

There pope and patriarch mutually agreed to "commit these excommunications to oblivion," but they also lamented that "this gesture of justice and mutual pardon is not sufficient to end both old and more recent differences between the Roman Catholic Church and the Orthodox Church."[45] Perhaps healing had begun, but multiple scars still remained. Humbert's words, spoken in anger, had proved truer than he knew in the end: "We have sensed here both a great good, whence we greatly rejoice in the Lord, and the greatest evil, whence we lament in misery."

RECOMMENDED READING

Barbero, Alessandro. *Charlemagne: Father of a Continent*. Berkeley: University of California Press, 2018.

Louth, Andrew. *Modern Orthodox Thinkers*. Downers Grove, IL: InterVarsity Press, 2015.

Meyendorff, John. *Byzantine Theology*. 2nd ed. New York: Fordham University Press, 1999.

Papadakis, Aristeides, and John Meyendorff. *The Christian East and the Rise of the Papacy: The Church AD 1071–1453*. Crestwood, NY: St. Vladimir's Seminary Press, 1993.

Runciman, Steven. *The Eastern Schism*. Oxford: Clarendon, 1955.

Ware, Timothy (Kallistos). *The Orthodox Church*. Baltimore: Penguin, 1963.

five

MARTIN LUTHER'S
NINETY-FIVE THESES (1517)

*"When our Lord and Master Jesus Christ said,
'Repent,' he willed the entire life of believers
to be one of repentance."*

With this sentence, a young Augustinian monk began proposing a set of theses for academic debate by his ecclesiastical superiors. He was worried about the abuse of money by leaders in the church. Especially, he wanted to protest the recent sales campaign of Johannes Tetzel, a Dominican friar who was raising money for the Fugger bank and the local archbishop, Albert of Brandenburg, by selling indulgences—money that would ultimately make its way back to Pope Leo X for the building of Saint Peter's Basilica in Rome. Surely, if the people in charge knew, he thought, they would do something.

They did something—but it was not exactly the something that the thirty-three-year-old Luther wanted.

Luther was not the first to call for reform in the way the medieval Western church was preaching, teaching, and living out the gospel. Cries for such reform had echoed down previous centuries, as we've read, and many in the early sixteenth century already wanted change. In Basel, humanist author Desiderius Erasmus (1466–1536) had just published a controversial Greek New Testament; in Glarus, priest Huldrych Zwingli (1484–1531) was reading it. But for better or worse, Luther's *Ninety-Five Theses*, meant for an academic debating hall, were what set off the thunderstorm that reshaped Western Christianity.[1]

WHERE WE ALL STARTED?

Some years ago, when I was in graduate school at Duke University, I was going over the course schedule with my mother on the phone and happened to mention that Duke offered a class on Luther. "Oh, you should take that one," she said. "That's where we all started." By *we* she meant Protestant *we*.

I entered the class with the picture many of us have in our heads: the quiet October Wednesday morning in 1517, the friar creeping to the door of All Saints' Church in Wittenberg and with one nail striking a death blow to medieval Catholicism. But by the end of the course I learned that the history of the Reformation was far more complex than I had previously expected.

First of all, we have no reason to believe that Luther actually nailed the theses to the door. We have no reason to believe he didn't, but the earliest report of the nailing comes from his friend Philip Melanchthon (1497–1560) after his death. The door "functioned as a bulletin board for various announcements related to academic and church affairs," so it's certainly possible he posted them; "whether or not Luther put the theses on the door, he certainly mailed them off that day to his superiors with an annoyed note."[2]

Luther had come to think that the church of his day had radically obscured the gospel. Part of this was political; the last several centuries had been a time of administrative papal turmoil.

In 1302, as part of a battle with secular rulers, Pope Boniface VIII had issued the bull *Unam Sanctam*, which claimed the pope had temporal as well as spiritual sovereignty over everyone. In response, King Philip IV of France (who had previously said that he was "nobody's vassal") forced the papal conclave to elect a French pope, Clement V, to succeed Boniface. Clement promptly refused to move to Rome; he set up his court, first at Poitiers, then in 1309 at Avignon, where seven other popes, all French, followed him. (Critics named the period the "Babylonian captivity" of the papacy as a parallel to the kingdom of Judah's captivity in actual Babylon in the sixth century BC.)

Finally, Gregory XI moved the papacy back to Rome in 1376. That did not end the conflict, however. When Gregory XI died in 1378, the conclave elected an Italian, Urban VI; this angered the French cardinals, who promptly elected a French cleric as Pope Clement VII instead—and he went back to Avignon. This touched off a tumultuous four decades during which at least two and sometimes three popes and "antipopes" were ruling (another faction began electing popes at Pisa) before the Council of Constance (1414–1418) put an end to the whole thing by getting everyone to agree to the election of Martin V in 1417.

This may have ended the immediate turmoil, but it did not end the continued growth of an "imperial" papacy in which popes behaved—and spent money—as if they were secular rulers clinging to secular thrones. This bothered Luther, as it bothered many other people in the late fifteenth and early sixteenth centuries. Soon he was uniting this complaint to a set of theological insights regarding the relationship between grace and good works: just as the church had obscured the gospel through the failure of its shepherds to shepherd their flock, he argued, it had also obscured the freedom of God's grace by allowing people to "earn" their salvation.

The school of theology that had shaped Luther's education was called the *via moderna*, a form of the philosophy called "nominalism." Originally taught by William of Ockham (c. 1287–1347), it had been transmitted to Luther's generation by Gabriel Biel (c. 1420–1495). According to Biel, even after the fall human beings had the natural ability to love God above everything else. By doing this, they fulfilled their side of the covenantal arrangement God had made. To anyone who loved God to the best of his or her ability God would give the supernatural grace required for salvation.

Late medieval Christians believed that every serious sin had three aspects: the guilt of the sin, the eternal penalty of separation from God, and the temporal disciplinary punishment that the sin deserved. When a sinner repented, God forgave the guilt and the eternal penalty, but the temporal penalty remained. Traditionally, it was worked off through acts of penance prescribed by the church. At first the punishment for serious sins could be extremely severe, and people tended to put off public repentance until late in life—like Constantine in our first chapter—because they weren't ready to take on the harsh discipline. For this reason the church came to impose lighter and lighter penances so as not to frighten people away from coming back to God.

But the church also thought that such relatively light penance didn't suffice to wipe away the temporal consequences of serious sin; temporal punishment not worked off in life would have to be atoned for in purgatory. God would forgive anyone who repented, even at the last split second. But such people would have to undergo incredible suffering in purgatory. Late medieval Christians became more worried about purgatory than about hell.

Indulgences, declarations by the church forgiving some or all of the temporal penalty owed by a person, were attached to activities like pilgrimages and almsgiving. The church taught that

Christ and the saints had laid up a vast treasury of holiness, and because of the communion of saints this holiness could be transferred to the "account" of Christians who met the requirements. Furthermore, indulgences earned by living Christians could be transferred to other Christians, living or dead. In practice, indulgences were often seen as "get-out-of-purgatory-free" tickets, which could be earned on behalf of dead relatives. And most notoriously, since giving alms was one good work to which indulgences were attached, indulgences could be used as a form of fund raising, as they were in that fateful autumn of 1517 in Saxony.

THE SPREAD OF THE FIRE

Luther wrote his theses in Latin, the language of theological debate at the time. They were printed on a broadside using a relatively new technology, the printing press. In addition to the copies sent to church officials, Luther gave a few to his friends.[3] There was no sign of any debate happening though. Then Albert of Brandenburg showed Luther's points to some other theologians. They "encouraged Albert to send a copy to Rome and demand action against Luther"—and Albert did.[4] Luther was called before Cardinal Cajetan at Augsburg in 1518 to answer for himself and found the interview so distressing that it upset his bowels.

Meanwhile, the theses had been translated into German. By early 1518 they were making their way around the countryside in theological language that even the common people could read. Tetzel even produced his own set of theses in response. In 1519, in Leipzig, Luther finally got the debate he wanted:

> The issue quickly became not indulgences, or even Tetzel's indulgences (which were extraordinary by any estimate), but the authority of the church: Did the pope have the right

to issue indulgences? The substance of the original matter—whether humans could draw on the treasury of Christ's merits, deposited with the church, to alter their standing with God—was of little concern to Luther's opponents. In fact, they were repeatedly forbidden to debate it with him. The question was instead whether the church could declare that it was so and rightly expect obedience.[5]

At Leipzig Luther famously announced that "a simple layman armed with Scriptures is to be believed above a pope or a council without it."[6] In 1520 he was threatened with excommunication in the bull *Exsurge Domine*. In response he wrote *The Address to the Christian Nobility*, *The Babylonian Captivity of the Church*, and *On the Freedom of a Christian*:

> With these three essays he set himself and his (by now) many sympathizers in opposition to nearly all the theology and practice of late medieval Christendom. In the first, he urged secular rulers to take the necessary reform of the church into their own hands, while arguing that all Christians were priests. In the second, he reduced the seven sacraments to three (baptism, the Lord's Supper, and penance), then to two, while radically altering their character. In the third, he told Christians they were free from the law (in particular the laws of the church) while they were bound in love to their neighbors.[7]

Not satisfied with his published attacks, Luther burned the bull and a copy of canon law for good measure in December; the pope responded by *actually* excommunicating Luther in *Decet Romanum Pontificem* (1521).

In response to all of this, Holy Roman Emperor Charles V (1500–1558) called a diet (meeting) at Worms. Though he ruled over the German parts of the Holy Roman Empire, Charles lived in his Spanish domains. He wanted to meet the many lords and princes of the German states. But he also wanted to deal with Luther. Luther still expected debate but instead was asked to recant. After considerable verbal fencing he announced:

> Unless I can be instructed and convinced with evidence from the Holy Scriptures or with open, clear, and distinct grounds of reasoning . . . then I cannot and will not recant, because it is neither safe nor wise to act against conscience.[8]

The diet condemned Luther. On the way home he was kidnapped—by his own ruler, Elector Frederick, who decided that was the best way to keep him safe. Luther stayed (unhappily) in Wartburg Castle for ten months under the guise of Junker Jörg. He began translating the Bible into German and writing commentaries and pastoral advice for people who were now asking whether the freedom of a Christian meant that they could leave monasteries and convents, and whether they should still confess their sins to a priest.

In 1522 Luther went back to Wittenberg without Frederick's permission and began preaching again. Eventually he married an escaped nun, Katharina von Bora (1499–1552). Legend has it that she and her monastic sisters were smuggled out of the convent in a merchant wagon.[9] The Luthers moved into the former Augustinian cloister in Wittenberg, where they hosted friends and students and took in boarders. Katie brewed beer and saw to the large household; in addition to all the visitors, they had six children, though some died young. Luther changed diapers, wrote hymns, issued the *Small Catechism* and *Large Catechism* (both in 1529) to teach the growing numbers of believers in his message, finished his translation of the entire Bible into German (in 1534), and issued increasingly savage treatises against his enemies as he grew older and crankier. In 1546 he died with a piece of paper in his pocket that said "We are beggars, that's the truth."[10]

THE REFORMATION OF THE CITIES

By the time Luther nailed up (or at least mailed off) his treatise, humanist and Bible translator Erasmus, the illegitimate son of a priest, had already published some of the books that would make him well known.[11] Humanist scholars, a circle that often but not always overlapped with reformers in the early sixteenth century, were those who were interested in reviving the classical learning of Greece and Rome but in a Christian context. Throughout his life, Erasmus translated the works of the church fathers, who he thought provided solutions to contemporary ills.

In 1519 Erasmus issued a revised edition of his Greek New Testament, maintaining its "dangerous" readings—such as Matthew 4:17: "From that time on Jesus began to preach, 'Repent (μετανοέω), for the kingdom of heaven has come near.'" The Latin Vulgate, translated by Jerome in the fourth century, had rendered this Greek word into Latin as "do penance" (*paenitentiam ago*). Luther had earlier recorded the impact of Erasmus's first edition on him: "It happened that I learned—thanks to the work and talent of the most learned men who teach us Greek and Hebrew with such great devotion—that the word *poenitentia* means *metanoia* in Greek."[12] Erasmus's friend Thomas Linacre supposedly remarked on reading the new edition, "Either this is not the gospel, or we are not Christians."[13] People began to say that "Erasmus laid the egg that Luther hatched," but Erasmus in fact regarded Luther as a dangerous radical.[14] There were even more radical reformers coming though.

In a movement scholars refer to as the Urban Reformation, these new ideas began to spread through many of Europe's great northern cities "with their wealthy merchants and urban aristocrats . . . the most dramatic growth was in the areas outside 'princely' control: the free imperial cities and the Swiss cantons."[15] People called those who held such ideas *evangelicals*, a word deriving from the Latin word for "gospel," *evangelion*. After 1529, they also began to become known as Protestants.

In 1519 Zwingli—who had become convinced of reforming ideals sometime after 1516 and had moved to Zurich to become a priest at the city's main church—discarded the church's lectionary schedule of Bible readings and began to preach through the book of Matthew. He was already a "people's priest," whose duties were mainly devoted to preaching in the vernacular; it was his abandonment of the lectionary that was scandalous. After that, he moved on to preach through other books. In 1522 he roasted sausages at the home of a local printer and ate them on a Sunday in Lent that was appointed for fasting. When challenged, he preached a sermon called "On the Choice and Freedom of Foods."

The city magistrates backed him up, and over the next few years Zurich abandoned many features of Catholic liturgy and practice. In 1525 they celebrated Maundy Thursday in German for the first time in a liturgy Zwingli designed: "Participants sat around tables; wooden bowls and plates were used for the sacrament; there was no organ music or singing; and the sermon took a central place."[16] Church attendance was made mandatory, and ordinances passed by the church ruled every aspect of life—from forbidding swearing to regulating gravestones to making sure no one laughed during the sermon.

Similar movements arose in other cities. For example, in Basel reform was led by priest and professor Johannes Oecolampadius (1482–1531) and in Strasbourg by humanist Martin Bucer (1491–1551), who became pastor of the city church, as well as by Matthäus Zell (1477–1548) and his wife Katharina Schütz Zell

(c. 1497–1562).[17] In these places the Mass was abolished and replaced by services in local languages, images were removed from churches, various kinds of schools were established to educate believers, and church life was regulated. (Bucer, for example, had "special wardens" installed in congregations to keep tabs on people's faith and practice.)

CAN WE SPEED UP THE PACE?

All this was still not fast enough for some. Long before Luther, German peasants had been unhappy with the state of things.[18] Worsening economic conditions in the late fifteenth century led to attempts by landowners to try to gain more money from peasants (a term that included not only farmers but miners and artisans—even small factory owners like Luther's father): "Grazing land, once available for all members of the community, was taken by the lord as his own property to be used for large-scale commercial farming. Further, peasants were denied traditional rights to fish and hunt, and rents went up steeply."[19] The *Bundschuh* revolts erupted, so called because the peasants had a traditional peasant shoe (*bundschuh*) on their banners.

The *Bundschuh* revolters gobbled Luther's treatises up. They were already arguing that the landowners were behaving unjustly. Luther gave them even more theological points with which to argue. In March 1525 one particular group of peasants incorporated Luther's theological points into a set of articles they drew up against their landowner opponents:

> The peasants demand that this Gospel be taught them as a guide in life, and they ought not to be called disobedient or disorderly. . . . Christ has delivered and redeemed us all, without exception, by the shedding of His precious blood, the lowly as well as the great. Accordingly, it is consistent with Scripture that we should be free and wish to be so.[20]

In addition to asking to be able once again to fish, hunt, and cut wood on their lords' land, they also demanded the right to appoint their own pastors. Luther was incensed. Their economic arguments might be all right, but they had no business using his theological arguments to undergird them: salvation by grace through faith "had nothing to do with hunting and fishing rights."[21]

The peasants began to transfer their allegiance to pastor Thomas Müntzer, a disciple of Luther's who had parted ways with him over the slow pace of reform and in 1524 published the anti-Luther pamphlet *A Highly Provoked Defense and Answer to the Spiritless, Soft-living Flesh at Wittenberg Who Has Most Lamentably Befouled Pitiable Christianity in a Perverted Way by His Theft of Holy Scripture*. (They really knew how to insult people in the sixteenth century!) Müntzer preached a sermon in favor of the peasants before Luther's patron Elector Frederick and led part of their armies in the revolt that followed. In 1525 they were soundly defeated at the battle of Frankenhausen. Meanwhile, Luther had published *Against the Murderous, Thieving Hordes of Peasants*, which called on the nobles to "knock down, strangle, and stab" the rebels. Over ten thousand peasants and their leaders died in the revolt, including Müntzer.

Meanwhile, all was not well in Zwingli's realm. Zwingli approved abandoning the Mass and removing images (statues, paintings, etc.) from churches, but he thought that the preaching of the gospel would lead people to peacefully do this on their own. Instead, riots broke out beginning in 1523. Eventually, the crowds were calmed and the rest of the art was removed quietly, but not until a lot of damage had been done.

Then in 1525 Conrad Grebel (c. 1498–1526) and Felix Manz (c. 1498–1527) began to hold secret meetings. They and their friends believed that "the name Christian could be applied only to those who truly followed Jesus, and not indiscriminately to all who were baptized"; in addition, they had become convinced that only adult baptism was valid.[22] At their first meeting after the Zurich city council outlawed their gatherings, they baptized each other, and soon began to baptize others in violation of the laws; in addition, they met to study the Bible, pray, and eat the Lord's meal.

This original gathering of what became known as the Anabaptist movement (from the Greek for "rebaptism," which is what their opponents thought they were doing) soon died out—Manz was executed by the Zurich city council in 1527. But the new reforms spread through the Swiss cantons, southern Germany, and Austria:

> A peasant carting his onions to market; a furrier plying his craft in north German towns; a housewife or nun to whom some new word about Christ or the saints raised questions about religious practice; a weaver or a shearer joining with fellow cloth makers in a Lowlands town; a schoolteacher whose natural theological curiosity pressed him to re-examine both Scripture and the Latin fathers—all of these and many more found themselves open to the new and strange words of itinerant Anabaptist missionaries. They spoke plainly to the common people and moved on to other towns and villages after only a few days of instructing new converts.[23]

Anabaptists rejected Catholic teaching, but they also rejected the close alliance between church and state typical of Luther, Zwingli, and Bucer's magisterial Reformation (so called because of its close alliance with the magistrates who ruled in cities and towns). Their disagreements over baptism were theological, but also political; to reject infant baptism meant rejecting the model of a cradle-to-grave Christian society. Anabaptists frequently shared their possessions communally, they refused to swear oaths to the secular state, they were often pacifists, and they drew many adherents from among those same peasants who had so frightened Luther.

In 1529 Charles V forbade both Zwinglianism and Anabaptism within his empire at the Diet of Speyer and decreed that Anabaptists should be executed as heretics. In Lutheran areas, this often happened by drowning, in cruel irony. Catholics, also unsympathetic, burned Anabaptists at the stake. Then in 1533 several Anabaptist extremists took over the city of Münster and declared that the apocalypse was coming and they could use violence to bring in God's kingdom. This included forcing baptism on people, instituting polygamy (the leader had sixteen wives), and forbidding all books but the Bible. The city was besieged, and the Anabaptist rebels were defeated in 1535.

This naturally alarmed the Anabaptists' opponents. It alarmed many Anabaptists as well; out of the chaos former priest Menno Simons (1496–1561) began to consolidate the movement and advocate pacifism—eventually giving his name to one of its largest branches, the Mennonites. In the late 1570s persecution ended in the Netherlands, Menno's home, but in some places Anabaptists were persecuted into the late 1600s.

The Lawyer Who Ruled a City

In France, Reformation ideas made a very different journey. There, in the early sixteenth century, a group of reform-minded French Catholic theologians known as the Circle of Meaux seized eagerly first on the humanism of Erasmus and then on the ideas of Luther.[24] They published pamphlets against indulgences and corruption and began translating the Bible into French. Many remained Catholic, but one, Guillaume Farel (1489–1565), began to believe that true reform entailed separation from Rome. This eventually led him to flee to Geneva, where in 1536 a young humanist reforming French lawyer named Jean Cauvin (1509–1564) showed up. Cauvin was author of a hot-off-the-presses theological pamphlet known as the *Institutes of the Christian Religion.* (The publication would lengthen in later editions.) We know him as John Calvin.

Calvin had begun by training to become a priest, but his father had steered him toward the law as being more lucrative. Sometime around 1529 or 1530, he began to be convinced of "Lutheran" ideas, and in 1533 he fled Paris along with his friend Nicolas Cop (1501–1540) after Cop delivered an address with "Lutheran" themes, which got him in trouble with the king of France. Farel and Calvin became friends.

Calvin had hoped to go on to a life of study in Basel, but Farel convinced his new friend to stay in Geneva and pastor those there who had become convinced of the new "evangelical" ideas:

> Farel detained me in Geneva, not so much by counsel and exhortation, as by a dreadful imprecation, which I felt to be as if God had from heaven laid his mighty hand upon me to arrest me. . . . And after having learned that my heart was set upon devoting myself to private studies for which I wished to keep myself free from other pursuits, . . . he proceeded to utter an imprecation that God would curse my retirement, and the tranquility of the studies which I sought, if I should withdraw and refuse to give assistance, when the necessity was so urgent.[25]

Calvin remained at first until 1539, when the magistrates kicked both him and Farel out and he went to Strasbourg to pastor French refugees. He returned after a change of magistrates and from 1541 until his death,

> Calvin and fellow pastors administered baptism and Communion; presided over marriages (which took place during

ordinary services); and managed public charity. They participated with church elders in the meetings of the renowned Consistory, which gathered every Thursday to censure, even excommunicate, believers guilty of offenses against Reformed morality or doctrine.[26]

Calvin also wrote a catechism and an order of worship that included the singing of the Psalter—a hallmark of worship in the Reformed tradition for years—and revised his *Institutes* in both French and Latin into the compendium of doctrine we know today. By the time he died, his approach was firmly entrenched in Geneva. It had begun to spread as well to France, the Netherlands, the Holy Roman Empire—and England.

Divorced, Beheaded, Died

To truly understand the arrival of the Reformed faith in England, we need to step back to the early 1530s.[27] At that point Henry VIII (1491–1547) had ruled as a Catholic king since taking the throne in 1509 at the age of seventeen; in 1521 he had even written a treatise against Luther's ideas, which won him the honorary title Defender of the Faith from Pope Leo X. But he was also attempting to divorce his wife of over twenty years, Catherine of Aragon.

Catherine had first been married to Henry's older brother, Arthur, the heir to the throne, but Arthur had died shortly after their 1505 marriage, making Catherine a young and inconvenient widow. When Henry became king, he agreed to marry his brother's widow, which required special dispensation from the pope. But after two decades Catherine had only borne Henry one legitimate surviving heir, a daughter, Mary (queens not being considered worthy rulers at the time), and he had fallen in love with a member of Catherine's court, Anne Boleyn, after conducting an affair with Anne's sister Mary. Catherine was forty, Henry thirty-four, and Anne twenty-five. Henry believed that if he could have his marriage to Catherine annulled and marry Anne, she would be able to bear him children for many years, including boys.

Henry does seem sincerely to have believed that in getting a papal dispensation to marry Catherine he had gone against Leviticus 20:2 and that this was one reason the two of them had no surviving sons. He appealed to Pope Clement VII on this basis. But Catherine was also the aunt of Holy Roman Emperor Charles V, who seems to have influenced the pope to make the request disappear into ecclesiastical limbo. Henry and his advisers took matters into their own hands.

In 1531 Catherine was banished from court, and in 1532 Henry appointed Thomas Cranmer (1489–1556) as archbishop of Canterbury. Cranmer pronounced the marriage annulled and married Henry to Anne. In 1533 Parliament declared Mary illegitimate, and in 1534 they declared that Henry VIII was "supreme head" of what was, at that point, a Catholic church in England in all but name. But it was not so for long.

Henry's famous succession of wives ("divorced, beheaded, died, divorced, beheaded, survived") happened for personal reasons but also political, dynastic, and religious ones. Anne was known to have Protestant sympathies; this was also true of most of Henry's other wives, with the exception of Catherine Howard. Henry dissolved monasteries in England between 1536 and 1541 so that he could have their considerable wealth for the Crown, and many of his advisers began to champion Protestantism as the preferable intellectual and devotional course. His chief counselor for many years, Thomas Cromwell (c. 1485–1540), supported Henry until he came to grief after arranging Henry's unsuccessful marriage to Anne of Cleves. A 1538 campaign by

Cromwell led to the destruction of saints' shrines and to the placing of a large Bible in every parish church in England. (Ironically, the translation was based on that of William Tyndale, who had been forbidden to translate the Bible into English in 1523 and executed in 1527 for refusing to support Henry's desire for an annulment.)

At Henry's death in 1547, his son by Jane Seymour, Edward VI (1537–1553) assumed the throne; he was only nine. During his brief reign of six and a half years, having been raised as a Protestant and being surrounded by Protestant advisers, he made England an indisputably Protestant country.[28] The Book of Common Prayer gave England a new Protestant liturgy, and Protestant articles of faith were drawn up. Edward also named a Protestant successor in his will—his cousin, Lady Jane Grey—since his heir otherwise would be his Catholic sister, Mary, restored to the line of succession by Parliament in 1544. Jane was proclaimed queen when Edward died, but her reign lasted only nine days before she was deposed and executed.

Mary (1516–1558) ruled England as a Catholic for five years, during which she imprisoned and eventually executed many Protestant leaders and exiled others; restored the articles of religion in place under Henry; sought out renewed relations with the papacy; encouraged Parliament to pass the "Statues of Repeal," which voided anti-Catholic legislation; appointed Reginald Pole as archbishop of Canterbury (he would be the last Catholic archbishop); and restored the Mass:

> Mary launched, against Pole's advice, a policy of severe repression against the Protestants. The privy council and Parliament went along with the queen because they had only expected a few heretics to be burned. They were taken aback when over two hundred and fifty perished in the flames.[29]

Mary also married Catholic monarch King Philip of Spain in 1554. But the marriage produced no children, and when Mary died in 1558 she knew she would be succeeded by her Protestant half sister, Elizabeth. Catholicism had become "identified in the minds of many Englishmen with bigotry, blood, and Spain."[30]

Elizabeth I (1533–1603) ruled for forty-five years. The church she established in what is known as the "Elizabethan Settlement" was Reformed, and it proclaimed again its independence from the pope in 1558, but it was not reformed in as thoroughgoing a fashion as Calvin had done in Geneva (or Zwingli in Zurich or Bucer in Strasbourg). It still possessed bishops consecrated by other bishops; worship proceeded according to the Book of Common Prayer, which was rooted in medieval liturgy; and traditional practices and vestments were allowed. The Thirty-Nine Articles that Parliament established for the church condemned Roman Catholicism in no uncertain terms but also condemned the practices of more radical Protestants.

NOT ALL ONE-SIDED

Up to this point, the bare outlines of the story of the Reformation may be familiar to you. What may be less familiar, and what would certainly have surprised my mother, is the reform *within* Catholicism in the same time period.[31] Those who came to be called Protestants were not offering their proposals in a vacuum. In fact, as discussed in the previous chapter, both lay and clergy had been asking for changes and seeking ways to deeper faith for over three hundred years. We can see this in the writings of great medieval saints such as Catherine of Siena (1347–1380), whose works include *Dialogue of Divine Providence*, a call to deeper spirituality, as well as sternly worded letters to the last Avignon pope, Gregory XI, encouraging him to move back to Italy; in the founding of the Franciscan and Dominican orders and lay movements such as the Beguines, Friends of God, and Brethren of the Common Life; and in the many councils called by the late medieval church in attempts at reform.[32]

In the sixteenth century, networks of reform developed in France, Italy, and Spain. In France, many members of the Circle of Meaux stayed Catholic, as did noblewoman and author Marguerite of Navarre (1492–1549), sister and wife to kings, who corresponded with Protestants like Calvin but never became one. In Spain, Bible studies formed that were suspected of being Protestant by the Inquisition but repeatedly insisted they were not. In Italy, Gasparo Contarini (1483–1542) responded positively to Lutheran ideas and promoted them in his preaching. Contarini was eventually made a cardinal by Pope Paul III, along with Reginald Pole and others whom the pope hoped would spur reform; but his resulting reform proposals in 1536 seemed too revolutionary.

In 1541, a dialogue took place between Catholic and Protestant representatives at Regensburg, but no agreement could be reached on the sacramental issues at stake. Though we may not realize it now, the sacraments were often the most controversial part of "Lutheran" teaching to Catholic thinkers. (Regensburg *was* able to reach agreement on justification by faith, for instance.) The next year, Gian Pietro Carafa (1476–1559)—who wished to reform moral standards but despised Protestant ideas—encouraged Paul III to establish the Roman Inquisition. Pole, the last of the more conciliatory cardinals, narrowly missed being elected pope in 1549 when Paul III died. Carafa eventually became Pope Paul IV in 1555.

Before Paul III died, however, he made one reform move with centuries of consequences; he finally called the general church council that Luther had asked for decades earlier. The council was meant to discuss ways to reform doctrine and practice and to respond to Protestant ideas. It met off and on at Trento (Trent) in Italy between 1545 and 1563. In general, Trent represented a serious attempt to deal with "ignorance, fornication, greedy careerism, and absenteeism" among Catholic clergy and to encourage good preaching and catechesis.[33] It also encouraged new reforming religious orders—the Jesuits, for example, whose official approval had just preceded the council in 1540—and new movements of reform within old orders, such as the Capuchins and Discalced Carmelites. The first, so called because they wore *cappuccios* (hoods), were a stricter form of Franciscans founded by Matteo de Bascio, who sought to return to Francis's ideals of poverty; the second was sparked by the desire for the stricter rule of life of Carmelite nun and mystic Teresa of Ávila (1515–1582), who founded a convent following this stricter rule and collaborated with Juan de Yepes—known in English as John of the Cross—to establish religious houses for men as well. (They were called *discalced*, meaning "barefoot," because they wore sandals.)

But Trent just as seriously staked out its theological positions on doctrinal positions like transubstantiation, liturgical practice, and clerical marriage in opposition to Protestant ones:

> The primacy of the pope survived a great challenge; the focus on bishops and priests serving local communities brought renewed attention to grassroots faith; the invention of seminaries gave new shape to the formation and education of clergy; and the church's patterns of doctrine and worship remained unchallenged until the equally monumental Second Vatican Council 400 years later.[34]

Where We're All Going

Like the schism between East and West, the events of the Reformation created fault lines between Christians that still reverberate.

It produced powerful new insights about grace and faith and Christian community—even as Christians broke communion with each other, convinced each other's insights on grace were incompatible and each other's practices of faith inadequate.

Ironically, by the time I finished that class on Luther all those years ago, I was able to reaffirm a bigger definition of *we*, one that includes all Christians. We all started together, two thousand years ago at the foot of the cross and at the door of the empty tomb. But we sometimes forget, and divisions that began five hundred years ago run deep. At such a time, it helps to remember that ultimately we are all saved by grace through faith, and to ponder that piece of paper in Luther's pocket when he died: "We are beggars, that's the truth."

Recommended Reading

Bainton, Roland. *Here I Stand.* New York: Abingdon, 1950.

Cameron, Euan. *The European Reformation.* Oxford: Oxford University Press, 2012.

Dickens, A. G. *The English Reformation.* University Park: Pennsylvania State University Press, 1991.

Duffy, Eamon. *The Stripping of the Altars.* New Haven, CT: Yale University Press, 2005.

Kittelson, James, and Hans Wiersma. *Luther the Reformer.* Minneapolis: Fortress, 2016.

Klaassen, Walter. *Anabaptism.* Waterloo, Ont.: Conrad Press, 1973.

MacCulloch, Diarmaid. *Reformation: A History.* New York: Penguin, 2003.

Muller, Richard. *The Unaccommodated Calvin.* Oxford: Oxford University Press, 2002.

Olin, John. *The Catholic Reformation.* New York: Fordham University Press, 1996.

O'Malley, John. *Trent and All That.* Cambridge, MA: Harvard University Press, 2000.

———. *Trent: What Happened at the Council.* Cambridge, MA: Belknap, 2013.

Payton, James. *Getting the Reformation Wrong.* Downers Grove, IL: InterVarsity Press, 2010.

Selderhuis, Herman J. *John Calvin: A Pilgrim's Life.* Downers Grove, IL: InterVarsity Press, 2009.

Spitz, Lewis. *The Protestant Reformation, 1517–1559.* Saint Louis, MO: Concordia, 2001.

Steinmetz, David C. *Calvin in Context.* 2nd ed. Oxford: Oxford University Press, 2010.

———. *Luther in Context.* 2nd ed. Grand Rapids, MI: Baker Academic, 2002.

———. *Reformers in the Wings.* 2nd ed. Oxford: Oxford University Press, 2004.

Stjerna, Kirsi Irmeli. *Women and the Reformation.* Malden, MA: Blackwell, 2009.

six

THE EDINBURGH CONFERENCE (1910)

"The church is confronted today, as in no preceding generation, with a literally worldwide opportunity to make Christ known."

I n the cold winter of early 1886 at Cornell University in up-
state New York, British cricket hero John Edward Kynaston
Studd (brother of even *more* famous cricket hero C. T. Studd)
came to lecture on a speaking tour. In the audience that day was
a twenty-year-old student preparing for a career in either the law
or his father's lumber business. He had, in fact, come late to the
lecture. As the door opened, he heard Studd proclaiming the
Scriptures for his talk, Jeremiah 45:5 and Matthew 6:33 in
the King James Version: "Seekest thou great things for thyself?
Seek them not." "Seek ye first the kingdom of God."[1]

The young man, John R. Mott (1865–1955), later said that "these
two passages fastened themselves into my memory like barbs. I
could not rid my mind of them."[2] He met with Studd, and he
began to think seriously about Christian missionary work. Eventually, he presided at the 1910 Edinburgh Missionary Conference,
became honorary president of the World Council of Churches,
and changed the course of twentieth-century Protestantism.[3]

OLD WORLDS AND NEW ONES

By moving directly from the Protestant and Catholic Reformations in the sentence that began the last chapter directly to the twentieth century in the sentence that begins this one, we seem at first to be skipping over a story many Christians are most fond of telling: the missionary spread of Protestantism in the seventeenth through nineteenth centuries. But there is a reason why this sentence, delivered by Mott to the opening session of the most famous Protestant missionary conference ever, was chosen to represent that story. It was the culmination of one set of missionary efforts and the beginning of new ones.

The sixteenth century hosted more than doctrinal debates and the divvying up of Europe's countries among Catholic, Lutheran, and Reformed allegiances; it was also an age of exploration and missionary effort.[4] Christianity has, of course, always been a global religion; from the time of Paul's first missionary journeys in Acts, it adapted to the many places it traveled, from England to Russia. It has also always been a missionary religion—whether the gospel was spread by whispers in catacombs or, regretfully, sometimes at the point of the swords of advancing armies. In the 1500s, as Europeans discovered lands new to them around the globe and the dueling Christian traditions that came out of the Reformation competed for adherents, Christianity ended up spreading to many new places.

The Age of Exploration had begun before the Reformation with late fifteenth-century voyages by the Portuguese to Africa and India—soon followed by the Spanish, French, English, and Dutch. Many of these voyagers set out mainly to spread power and open trade routes, but that did not mean they were entirely free of a desire to convert the new groups of people they met. When Columbus landed in the Bahamas in 1492, he claimed the islands as the property of his Spanish patrons, but he also expressed a desire to spread Christianity—coupled with a mis-understanding of the religious practices of those he met:

> I could see that they were people who would be more easily converted to our Holy Faith by love than by coercion, and wishing them to look on us with friendship I gave some of them red bonnets and glass beads which they hung round their necks, and many other things of small value, at which they were so delighted and so eager to please us that we could not believe it. . . . They appeared to me to be a very poor people in all respects. . . . I believe they would readily become Christians; it appeared to me that they have no religion.[5]

This encounter set the template for many that followed and has produced legacies the Christian West is still untangling: a sincere desire to spread the gospel coupled with a regretful identification of that gospel with Western civilization.

Both Catholics and Protestants continued to send missionaries into these new-to-them lands. Catholic missionary efforts were frequently spearheaded by the Jesuits; directly obedient to the pope, they were available to go wherever in the world he wanted to send them. Francis Xavier (1506–1552) and later Matteo Ricci (1552–1610) in Asia and Jean de Brébeuf (1593–1649) in North America were among the most famous Jesuits who set out. And English and Dutch Protestants established colonies in North America. (The Puritans, of course, are the most famous example of this.)

But even as the Christian message spread, it was being challenged.

THE LONG EIGHTEENTH CENTURY

During the centuries separating the Age of Exploration from the cold winter day at Cornell when John Mott heard J. E. K.

Studd, two things happened at the same time in the West. The first was that, for the first time since Christianity became the official religion of the Roman Empire, a widespread movement arose among cultural elites and governments questioning Christianity's prominence, truth, and cultural favor. This movement—commonly called the Enlightenment—developed out of an expansion of scientific discoveries that had begun in the sixteenth century.[6] Later historians and scientists would term these discoveries, beginning with the work of Nicolaus Copernicus (1473–1543), the Scientific Revolution, seeing in them a profound alteration of the way humans understood themselves in relationship to the universe.

At the time, the thinkers involved—many of whom were Christians—might not have described it that dramatically.[7] They felt that, as Galileo Galilei (1564–1642) explained, they were exploring God's book of nature just as Christians had historically explored the book of Scripture: "The holy Bible and the phenomena of nature proceed alike from the divine Word, the former as the dictate of the Holy Ghost and the latter as the observant executrix of God's commands."[8] In fact, they called themselves natural philosophers; the term *scientist* was not invented until 1833.

Still, it was true that a new emphasis was placed on observing nature in order to draw conclusions. (Later thinkers would call this the "scientific method.") And new conclusions were drawn, including Copernicus's groundbreaking conclusion that observations of the sky gave evidence that the earth revolved around the sun rather than vice versa. The period is often thought to conclude in 1687 with Isaac Newton's (1642–1727) composition of *Principia*, which laid down mathematic laws of gravity and motion that would shape human understanding of how the world worked until Einstein came along. However, the century that followed continued to see new experiments and the foundation of many scientific societies.

Of course, it was possible to explore the book of nature without exploring the book of Scripture, or to draw conclusions from the first that might undermine the second. A focus on human experience and reason as the chief sources of knowledge, and a distrust of traditional sources of knowledge (like the Bible) and authority (like monarchy and the papacy) characterized the writings of seventeenth-century thinkers such as René Descartes (1596–1650) and John Locke (1632–1704) and eighteenth-century ones like Voltaire (pen name of François-Marie Arouet; 1694–1778), David Hume (1711–1776), and Jean-Jacques Rousseau (1712–1778):

> The thinkers of the Enlightenment turned their backs on the past, turned their faces resolutely to the future, and looked forward to ever better things to come. Among those things was a new era of liberty, equality, and fraternity. Religion and monarchy would no longer shackle the human spirit. Freedom of expression and freedom of the press were rights that could not be denied. No more religious dogma, for Reason was the only god to be adored. No more hierarchy or privilege by reason of birth. No more kings—or at least no more kings without severe constitutional restraints.[9]

The American Revolution and the French Revolution did away with kings quite dramatically. The new United States declared itself independent of the British monarchy in 1776 and established a republic governed by elected officials along political and economic lines in tune with Enlightenment thought.[10] The American Founding Fathers drank deeply from the wells of deism, the idea that there was a God who had put the world in motion but did not intervene in it in any miraculous way. As one historian remarked:

[Benjamin] Franklin responded that Jesus had taught the best system of morals and religion that "the world ever saw." But on the troublesome question of the divinity of Jesus, he had along with other deists "some doubts." . . . [Jefferson] rejected the divinity of Jesus (as he believed Jesus did) and denounced the idea of the Trinity as "mere abracadabra," the saddest example of what happens when one trades "morals for mysteries, Jesus for Plato."[11]

France too declared a republic in 1792, though they killed their king as a result, and endured a great deal of turmoil (including the brief reigns of two different emperors and the slightly longer restoration of the original monarchy's heirs) before permanently becoming a republic in 1870. Throughout the nineteenth century, European countries and their overseas colonies attempted—some successfully, some unsuccessfully—to organize on democratic principles that included attention to the consent of the governed, the ability to vote, and freedom of religious practice from state interference. The way this transpired in France and Italy in particular would frighten the dethroned Roman Catholic Church for generations, and we'll pick up that story in the next chapter.

In a world devoid of state-enforced religion, where the best minds of the day were as likely to be deists or agnostics as not, what place was there for Christianity? Would it recover the missionary fervor of the early church? Spoiler alert: it would.

GREATLY AWAKENED, POWERFULLY SENT

Deists and revolutionaries were not the only ones who questioned the "Christendom" model, by which Christianity enjoyed state support and official protection. Devout Christians wondered if this was really the best way for the faith to grow and spread—and this sparked the second great development: revival. In seventeenth-century Lutheranism, pastor Philipp Jakob Spener (1635–1705) picked up on themes that had been prominent during the Middle Ages in his *Pia Desideria* (1675), which urged ordinary laity to pursue a serious faith through prayer, Christian conversation, and the study of Scripture.[12] Spener's writings influenced prominent nobleman Count Zinzendorf and his followers, known as the Moravians.

In England and its colonies, various protests also arose against the establishment and perceived "deadness" of Anglicanism, Congregationalism, and Presbyterianism. Several famous preachers are particularly associated with the revival that flourished from the 1720s to the 1740s: Anglicans John Wesley (1703–1791) and his brother Charles (1707–1788), influenced by the Moravians, in Britain; Congregationalist Jonathan Edwards (1703–1758) in the North American colonies; and George Whitefield (1714–1770), another Anglican priest who could be described as a "frenemy" of the Wesley brothers, in both places.[13]

In the colonies, proponents called this new movement the Great Awakening; in Britain, the Evangelical Revival. In both places it focused on the issues that had animated Spener—personal faith in Christ, prayer, Scripture reading, fellowship with other believers—and frequently added dynamic conversion-oriented preaching and emotional, physically demonstrative conversions. People fainted, wept, prayed, and sang enthusiastic hymns. Evangelists witnessed to the lower classes outside of traditional state-church power structures. The older more established denominations were torn by controversy over this "enthusiasm." About fifty years later, a second set of revivals swept the now-independent United States; many termed it the Second Great Awakening. It benefited the Methodists and Baptists in particular, who grew rapidly, and it caused the formation of new groups such as the Stone-Campbell movement (Christian Churches/Churches of Christ/Disciples of Christ).[14]

Meanwhile in England, among those who had left the Church of England under revival influence was a shoemaker named William Carey (1761–1834).[15] He ended up becoming a preacher among a group of Particular Baptists (essentially, strongly Calvinist Baptists); they were deep in debate as to whether it was appropriate to actively engage in missions. The most famous story about the controversy may be apocryphal but represents common sentiment:

> When a Baptist association meeting sought topics for discussion, Carey proposed his growing passion: "Whether the command given to the apostles to teach all nations was not binding on all succeeding ministers to the end of the world." "Young man, sit down, sit down!" was the reported response of one minister. "You are an enthusiast. When God pleases to convert the heathen, he'll do it without consulting you or me. Besides there must be another Pentecostal gift of tongues!"[16]

Carey disagreed. He soon wrote *An Enquiry into the Obligations of Christians, to Use Means for the Conversion of the Heathens*, published in 1792, arguing:

> As our blessed Lord has required us to pray that his kingdom may come, and his will be done on earth as it is in heaven, it becomes us not only to express our desires of that event by words, but to use every lawful method to spread the knowledge of his name.[17]

In October 1792, he had convinced his friends to form a missionary society, the Particular Baptist Society for the Propagation of the Gospel Amongst the Heathen.[18] By January 1793

Carey had volunteered to go as a missionary himself, and by November of that year he was in India.

Two hundred years before, John Calvin had sent missionaries to Latin America. Zinzendorf had been known for sending missionaries. The Wesleys had even served a term as missionaries. But something about Carey's effort caught public attention and inspired the founding of "an explosion of mission agencies" in Europe and North America and an explosion of Protestant missionaries across the globe, so that the very word *missionary* generally came to mean "a [Protestant] Westerner going to Asia, Africa, and Latin America."[19] Despite some struggles with male-dominated mission agencies, this soon came to include single female missionaries as well, who often taught in schools, worked in hospitals, and evangelized female-only spaces in the countries they went to. By 1900, there were about fifteen thousand European and American Protestant missionaries in the field:

> In 1800, perhaps 1 percent of Protestant Christians lived in Asia, Africa, and Latin America. By 1900, this number had grown to 10 percent. Today [in the late twentieth century], at least 67 percent of all active Protestant Christians live in countries once considered foreign mission fields. . . . Only 200 years ago, Protestant Christianity was almost exclusively Western. Now Protestants are strongest in Asia, Africa, and Latin America. From a Christian standpoint, the modern missionary movement has turned the world upside down.[20]

The more missionaries that were sent, the more the missionaries and sending agencies realized that their aims would be better fulfilled if they cooperated more explicitly. In 1854, Protestant missionaries held the first-ever international conference on the subject in New York.[21] The London Missionary Society held an explicitly ecumenical conference around the subject of missions in 1888, the Centenary Conference on the Protestant Missions of the World; 1,579 delegates from ten countries, representing 139 different denominations and other groups, were in attendance.[22] Twelve years later in 1900 a similar conference was convened in New York and drew record crowds.

Organizers began to plan for a Protestant conference to be called the Third Ecumenical Missionary Conference. But, recognizing that, as one Anglican clergyman involved with the planning said, the word *ecumenical* "cannot be used truthfully while great sections of the Church are in no way connected with the Conference," it was renamed the World Missionary Conference.[23] The 1,215 delegates were all Protestant (one Catholic sent an unofficial letter of greeting), and only twenty of them came from non-Western countries.[24] But, ironically, the new name would make the conference seem more far-reaching than the old.

NOT LIKE YOUR CHRIST

Eight commissions spent two years preparing reports for the conference, focusing specifically on problems and issues arising on the mission field—the magnitude of the evangelistic task, educating and preparing missionaries, relating missions to local churches and to governments, relationship to non-Christian faiths, and missionary cooperation.[25] On June 14, 1910, delegates finally gathered at the General Assembly Hall of the Church of Scotland in Edinburgh, first for an afternoon business meeting and then for an evening session, which began with the singing of "All People That on Earth Do Dwell" and included greetings from the king and an address by the president of the conference, Alexander Hugh Bruce, Sixth Lord Balfour of Burleigh. It was not Lord Balfour's words that were most remembered, however. The next morning, June 15, Methodist layman and delegate Mott was elected to preside over the conference—and there he stayed, for most of the rest of the eleven days.

From his days at Cornell hearing J. E. K. Studd, Mott had pursued a career with the YMCA. At this point he had been secretary of the Intercollegiate YMCA of the USA and Canada, and also secretary to the executive committee of the Student Volunteer Movement for Foreign Missions, for twenty-two years. In 1893 he had helped establish a Protestant cooperative venture, Foreign Missions Conference of North America, and in 1900 he had published his most famous book, *The Evangelization of the World in This Generation.* He had also helped plan the conference:

> He was the one . . . who decided, almost independently, that the 1910 Edinburgh meeting would not be a church leaders' meeting, as back in 1900, but rather a mission leaders' meeting, to focus on strategy rather than on mobilization.[26]

Mott was also chairperson of the commission on Carrying the Gospel to All the Non-Christian World, and it was in this capacity on that June morning that he delivered the sentence with which this chapter began.[27] His speech, drawing on the commission's research, outlined the sources of this opportunity: advances in technology, improved knowledge of non-Christian lands by Western Christians, and a perceived openness to the gospel in other countries—especially among lower classes poorly served by their own faiths and cultures.

But, he added on behalf of the commission, there was an urgency. Secularism and Modernism were also on the rise, at home and abroad, and missionaries needed to distance themselves from Western corruption:

> It is not strange, therefore, that the following challenge is a typical expression of the opinion of a great multitude of Asiatics and Africans: "You come to us with your religion.

You degrade our people with drink. You scorn our religion, in many points like your own, and then you wonder why Christianity makes such slow progress among us, I will tell you: It is because you are not like your Christ."

As the corrupt influences which have been mentioned constitute a deadly gift from the modern civilisation of the West, it is doubly incumbent on the Church to supply the antidote to such evil influences and to spread itself more widely among the people.[28]

The conference, after entertaining reports from all the commissions and debating practical questions, concluded on June 23 with prayer, Scripture reading, and the singing of "For All the Saints Who from Their Labors Rest" and "His Name Forever Shall Endure."[29] But it also did something that the previous missionary gatherings of its type had not (though several of them had thought it might be a good idea). To carry on the work of the conference, the Edinburgh meeting established a journal, the *International Review of Mission*, and a Continuation Committee, a committee "which gave birth to some of the most important Protestant internationalist structures of the twentieth century."[30]

INTO ALL THE WORLD, TOGETHER WITH ALL THE PEOPLE

The most immediate successor of the Continuation Committee was the International Missionary Council, founded in 1921. Mott became secretary of this council in 1928 and served until 1946. The IMC continued to hold world missionary conferences approximately every ten years, beginning in 1928 in Jerusalem; one feature of the IMC was a greater attention to holding meetings all over the globe. It proved that the attitude toward overseas mission was changing:

The first world war provoked by "Christian" countries had profoundly challenged the ideal of the Western civilization as embodiment of the gospel. The communist revolution of 1917 had made the dream of evangelizing the whole world within one generation unrealistic. At the Jerusalem conference, mission was strongly debated. Two major questions came up on which no real consensus emerged: the relation between the Christian message and other religions, and the theological interpretation of Christian social and political involvement.[31]

Another of the delegates at Edinburgh had been an Episcopal bishop, Charles Brent (1862–1929), consecrated by the US church for mission work in the Philippines. He addressed the conference twice during its proceedings, on one occasion seeking to remind the delegates that there was no true cooperation in mission without taking Roman Catholicism into account.[32] It has been often stated that he conceived of the idea of an ecumenical organization on church unity while he was in attendance at Edinburgh. There is no direct evidence of this, but when he returned and attended a meeting of his own denomination a few months later, he recorded in his diary that the idea of an organization devoted to "faith and order" sprang into his mind at a morning Eucharist service. No doubt all he had heard and said at Edinburgh was still fresh in his mind.[33]

It took almost two more decades, but Brent was the chief architect of the First World Conference on Faith and Order, which met in Lausanne, Switzerland, in 1927. Over four hundred delegates came from over one hundred Protestant denominations.[34] Brent died in 1929, but Faith and Order lived on; another conference was held in 1937.

Meanwhile Brent's colleague and friend Nathan Söderblom (1866–1931), archbishop of the Church of Sweden, had organized

yet another conference on cooperation in 1925. Leaving questions of faith and order to Brent's group, Söderblom's conference—
the World Conference of Life and Work—hoped to discuss the
relationship of the church to industrialization, work, and class
conflict. The official invitation expressed a hope that "the fa-
therhood of God and the brotherhood of all peoples will become
more completely realized through the church of Christ."[35] Another meeting was held in 1938.

At the second meetings of these two groups, it was decided that
they should merge. The actual merger was delayed until after
World War II, finally taking place in 1948 at Amsterdam; the new
organization was named the World Council of Churches. W. A.
Visser 't Hooft, a Dutch theologian and author, became the first
general secretary.[36] But there was one man everyone wanted to
honor. He had been involved with both the Life and Work and
Faith and Order conferences, had been provisional president of
the WCC before its actual formation, was a colleague of both
Brent and Visser 't Hooft, and incidentally had also won the Nobel
Peace Prize in 1946. Oh—and he had also made a speech long ago
in Scotland about the evangelization of the world in this generation. He was named lifelong honorary president of the new organization. It will be no surprise that his name was John R. Mott.

MISSIONS AND MODERNITY

Surprisingly to some, Eastern Orthodox groups began joining
the World Council of Churches in 1955—although the idea for
such a council of churches had also been proposed by the Ecumenical Patriarch of Constantinople in 1920 in a letter to "all the
churches of Christ" and had been another influential factor in
the plans of Mott and his colleagues.[37] A few years after Mott's
death, his IMC officially became part of the WCC in 1961, becoming its Division of World Mission and Evangelism.

Today there are 350 member churches in the WCC, although as yet the Roman Catholic Church is not one of them. (We'll explore its own response to secularism, modernity, and the missionary movement in the final chapter.) Many evangelical groups have raised questions about the political and theological attitudes of the WCC and its predecessors as well and have chosen to cooperate through other avenues such as the National Association of Evangelicals in the United States, founded in 1942, and the World Evangelical Alliance, founded as the World Evangelical Fellowship in 1951.[38]

Whether in the WCC or out of it, most churches have had a growing awareness that many of the issues raised as a result of exploration, Enlightenment, industrialization, revival, and world mission have yet to be resolved. The church is still confronted with the opportunity—and the challenge—of making Christ known. It would behoove us as we do to remember those two verses that so animated Mott: "Seekest thou great things for thyself? Seek them not." "Seek ye first the kingdom of God."

RECOMMENDED READING

Fagan, Brian. *Fish on Friday: Feasting, Fasting, and the Discovery of the New World.* New York: Basic Books, 2006.

Finke, Roger, and Rodney Stark. *The Churching of America 1776–2005.* New Brunswick, NJ: Rutgers University Press, 2005.

Hall, David. *Worlds of Wonder, Days of Judgment.* Cambridge, MA: Harvard University Press, 1990.

Heitzenrater, Richard. *Wesley and the People Called Methodists.* Nashville: Abingdon, 2013.

Hopkins, Charles Howard. *John R. Mott: A Biography.* Grand Rapids, MI: Eerdmans, 1979.

Lindberg, David, and Ronald Numbers, eds. *God and Nature: Historical Essays on the Encounter Between Christianity and Science.* Berkeley: University of California Press, 1986.

Marty, Martin E. *Pilgrims in Their Own Land: 500 Years of Religion in America*. New York: Penguin, 1984.

Neill, Stephen. *A History of Christian Missions*. New York: Penguin, 1994.

Tucker, Ruth. *From Jerusalem to Irian Jaya: A Biographical History of Christian Missions*. Grand Rapids, MI: Eerdmans, 2004.

seven

THE SECOND VATICAN COUNCIL (1962–1965)

"Hence this Second Vatican Council, having probed more profoundly into the mystery of the Church, now addresses itself without hesitation, not only to the sons of the Church and to all who invoke the name of Christ, but to the whole of humanity."

I remember very well my childhood growing up in the Methodist church in northern Indiana. They were happy days—my father was the pastor and served several different churches. I had friends and enjoyed Sunday school and sang in the choir. We took Communion once a quarter, using a pattern of worship that dated back to John Wesley and before him to the English Reformation: it was a solemn, quiet service full of sixteenth-century language with much time for individual contemplation. We sang from a hymnal containing many old European Protestant favorites from the Reformation to the present day; sometimes we sang gospel hymns from a gospel songbook. We were kind to Roman Catholics when we encountered them, but we didn't seek them out to plan activities or to worship with.

When I was in college, much of that changed. The denomination published a new hymnal and a new liturgy. The new liturgy had new language that sounded much more everyday and was based on the same model that the Roman Catholics nearby used. We were encouraged to celebrate Communion more frequently, to call it Eucharist, and to use real bread and real wine in place of wafers and individual cups of grape juice. We were told the service was to be upbeat and joyous and reminded that the Greek word *eucharistia* means "to give thanks." The new hymnal had songs from across the globe, from well before the Reformation, and from Catholic and Orthodox sources.

What happened? The short answer is, Vatican II. But why did a gathering of Roman Catholic leaders at the Vatican to deal with the problems of modernity in their own context have such a far-reaching impact? How did a meeting in Rome in the 1960s reach all the way to rural Methodists in Indiana in the 1980s? Thereby hangs a tale.[1]

MODERN PROBLEMS

Throughout history, church councils have been called to deal with pressing theological, political, and cultural issues. This was the case all the way back when Nicaea was summoned by Constantine in the fourth century (chap. 2). It was also the case nearly twenty councils later, in the calling of Trent by Paul III in the sixteenth century (chap. 5). Trent set Catholicism on a course it would follow for centuries—creating what we frequently now call Tridentine Catholicism. (*Tridentum* is the Latin name of the city of Trent.)

Since Trent, only one additional council had been called, the First Vatican Council. It was the first church council to be held in the Vatican—previous councils in Rome had been held at the

Lateran Basilica—and it was called in 1868 by Pius IX. Pius and his colleagues were struggling with the results of the Enlightenment, the American and French Revolutions, industrialization, the growth of missionary endeavors, and a steadily growing secularism in European society and government. The term *modernity* became "a handy catchword for summing up what was at stake."[2] How could these trends be addressed, and what guidance could be offered for faithful Catholics?

The council officially convened in December 1869 and met until July 1870. During a summer break in the meetings, the Franco-Prussian War began; French troops, who had been protecting the Vatican from Italian forces, returned home to fight. Pius, besieged in the Vatican by Italian troops, adjourned the council indefinitely. (It would not officially be declared over for another ninety years!)[3]

During its brief meeting, though, it produced two documents that it hoped would meet the challenges of a secularizing world: *Dei Filius,* a summary of Catholic teaching that condemned Modernism and rationalism, and *Pastor Aeternus,* which emphasized the pope's primacy over bishops and councils. It defined explicitly the long-assumed doctrine of "papal infallibility" when the pope exercised his teaching authority in issues relating to faith and morals:

> We teach and define as a divinely revealed dogma that when the Roman pontiff speaks EX CATHEDRA, that is, when, in the exercise of his office as shepherd and teacher of all Christians, in virtue of his supreme apostolic authority, he defines a doctrine concerning faith or morals to be held by the whole church, he possesses . . . that infallibility which the divine Redeemer willed his church to enjoy in defining doctrine concerning faith or morals.[4]

A few years later Pius's successor Leo XIII issued the influential papal encyclical *Aeterni Patris* (1879), attacking modern
philosophy and commending

> the philosophy and theology of Thomas Aquinas . . . as "the
> special bulwark and glory of the Catholic Faith." The intel-
> lectual system of Neo-Thomism, built on Aquinas's
> teachings, claimed to represent timeless, fixed, objective
> truth drawn from two sources: rational inquiry into the
> created, natural world and the supernatural truth revealed
> by God in Scripture and tradition.[5]

In 1893, Leo condemned new methods of biblical scholarship in
Providentissimus Deus. And in 1907, the Holy Office (the Vatican
department responsible for protecting Catholic teaching) released *Lamentabili*, a document explicitly condemning a number
of things they saw modern thinkers embracing—the use of
historical-critical biblical study, dependence on reason, and the
process of historical change.[6]

For many Catholics as the nineteenth century gave way to the
twentieth, such condemnations and affirmations represented
"refuge from the chaos" of modern materialism, war, and atheism
and allowed them to experience and preach a "confident, assertive
Catholicism."[7] Grounded in long-standing theological systems
and worshiping according to familiar rhythms of the Latin Mass,
a liturgy that had been basically unchanged since Trent, many no
doubt expected that things would go on just as they were.

But you've read my Methodist story already, so you know that
they were wrong.

THE NEW THEOLOGY IS ACTUALLY VERY OLD

In the early twentieth century, some Catholic thinkers began to
question how well Vatican I in particular and the concentration

of authority in the papacy in general (called *ultramontanism*) had *actually* dealt with the challenges facing the church.[8] Might it not be better, some of these theologians, philosophers, and biblical scholars wondered, if the church attempted to engage and understand the modern world and to speak eternal truth to modern problems? Protestants were doing similar things as they wrestled with the aftermath of the "Great War" and the devastation it had wrought—a devastation that seemed to dim some of the optimistic hopes we saw expressed in chapter six. The works of pastor-theologians like Karl Barth (1886–1968) and Dietrich Bonhoeffer (1906–1945), the latter eventually martyred by the Nazis, asked people to look anew at the God revealed in the Scriptures and to reckon with the reality of sin.

As they wrestled with these issues, Catholic scholars began to be interested in looking to the church fathers for inspiration. The Roman Catholic approach at the turn of the twentieth century was, like the Protestant one, set up to cope with the world of "Christendom": it presumed a nominally Christian society, with professedly Christian rulers, operating at least officially on Christian principles. But the earliest church fathers and mothers had been thinking and writing and evangelizing in a world that looked a lot more like the twentieth century—amid war and pagan philosophy, in the last days of empire. Perhaps there was something to be learned from looking at how they did it.

Ironically, some of the seeds of this renewal came from the very hierarchy officially opposed to such questioning. For example, the 1833 founding of the monastery of Solesmes, though initiated by supporters of a strong papacy, had led to a revival of interest in early church models of liturgy and music. Then, in 1905 Pius X officially encouraged devout believers to receive the Eucharist every week—this had been the case in the early church but not for over a thousand years.

New sources became available as well. Liturgical scholars encouraged translations of the liturgy into local languages so that worshipers in the pews could follow along and understand what the priest was saying in Latin. They used the *Patrologia Latina* (published between 1844 and 1864) and the *Patrologia Graeca* (1856–1866), new editions of the church fathers compiled by priest Jacques Paul Migne, who had sought to raise the education level of both priests and laity.

In the 1930s, efforts to renew, look back, and engage modernity began to center on the scholasticate (seminary) in Fourvière-Lyon, where theologian Henri de Lubac (1896–1991) lived, and at the University of Lyons, where he taught. Along with one of his students, Jean Daniélou (1905–1974), he began to issue an edition of the church fathers in French and released several ground-breaking books that engaged with modern theology, including *The Mystical Body* (1944).[9] Even more famous was his student, Hans Urs von Balthasar (1905–1988), who began to study and write extensively about the Eastern fathers. Another group of theologians coalesced around the Dominican seminary Le Saulchoir, where Marie-Dominique Chenu (1895–1990) and Yves Congar (1904–1995) composed works that encouraged greater ecumenism and an openness to historical change. One of Chenu's books, *Saulchoir: A School of Theology* (1937) was condemned as Modernist and placed on the Index of Forbidden Books.[10]

Like many movements, this one ended up being named by its critics. In 1946 a professor at the Pontifical University of Saint Thomas Aquinas in Rome, Réginald Garrigou-Lagrange, wrote an article condemning many of these authors, called "The New Theology: Where Is It Leading Us?"[11] The French term for "new theology," *nouvelle théologie*, stuck as a unifying term for this whole set of authors, even though many of them called what they were doing *ressourcement*—"return to the sources."

So far, though, this was a debate among academics. But all of that was about to change.

Fresh Air and the Crab on the Altar

Pius XII released *Humani Generis* in 1950, a condemnation of Modernism that resulted in crackdowns on leading *nouvelle* theologians. But when he died in 1958, he was succeeded by John XXIII, who called informally for an ecumenical council only a few months after his election as pope and summoned the meeting officially in 1961. When questioned as to why—his action caught everyone by surprise—he reportedly said that he wanted to "open the windows [of the church] and let in some fresh air."[12]

The council was a huge bureaucratic undertaking. It took over three years to prepare for it; some of the formerly disgraced *nouvelle* theologians were put on the preparatory planning committee. It had over two thousand participants, eleven working commissions, three secretariats, a number of handpicked experts for consultation, and eventually over a hundred observers from Protestant and Orthodox churches—John's invitation to these "outsiders" was a surprise as well. While more lay Catholic men were invited as the council went on, it took two years for any women to be invited as auditors (who could not vote), and even then only a total of twenty-three women were invited.

The council began officially in October 1962:

> At 8:30 in the gradually clearing morning light of October 11, 1962, the procession began to make its way across the great piazza, now thronged with an applauding, sometimes cheering, crowd. . . . Some 2,500 council fathers, fully vested in flowing white garments with white miters atop their heads, descended the great staircase of the palace next to the

church and seemed to flow from it through the piazza into St. Peter's. The Swiss Guards, the Noble Guards, the Palatine Guards, the bishops and patriarchs from the Eastern Catholic churches in their exotic vestments and crowns, and sundry others added color and variety to the scene.[13]

Suspended briefly when John died in June 1963, the council was continued by his successor Paul VI and ultimately concluded in December 1965.

Vatican II's deliberations were long and complex, its bureaucracy constantly shifting, and the documents that it issued many. But the overarching themes were the same ones that had animated the *nouvelle* theologians: the modern church needed to engage honestly with the modern world, and Scripture and the early church formed its best resources in doing so. The most important documents that emerged from the council were the four "constitutions" it produced: on the liturgy, on the theology of the church, on divine revelation, and on the place of the church in the modern world.

Sacrosanctum Concilium, the constitution on the liturgy, came first in 1963. Picking up on reforms from earlier in the century, it aimed to curb the practice for many centuries of people carrying on personal devotional time while the Mass was being said in Latin: "Mother Church earnestly desires that all the faithful should be led to that fully conscious, and active participation in liturgical celebrations which is demanded by the very nature of the liturgy."[14]

To aid in this, liturgical revisions were encouraged, and the charge given that these should devote greater prominence to Scripture and preaching and to the common prayer of the congregation. (*Dei Verbum*, the constitution on divine revelation, in addition to affirming both modern biblical scholarship and a greater attention to the interpretations of the church fathers, also called for more attention to Scripture in the liturgy.) Sacred music was to incorporate more music from around the world; sacred art for sanctuaries was to be less ornate. At one point *Sacrosanctum Concilium* stated:

> Particular law remaining in force, the use of the Latin language is to be preserved in the Latin rites.
>
> But since the use of the mother tongue, whether in the Mass, the administration of the sacraments, or other parts of the liturgy, frequently may be of great advantage to the people, the limits of its employment may be extended.[15]

There a Pandora's box was opened. The church published a revision of the liturgy in 1970 in Latin—most commonly called the *Novus Ordo* or "new order"—but meanwhile *Sacrosanctum Concilium* had become the basis for many, many permissions being granted to use local vernacular languages. The celebration of the Latin Mass disappeared, it seemed, almost overnight. Although it is possible today to find Catholic churches that celebrate the Mass in Latin, if you pick one at random and go in, it probably won't be doing so.

For those who approved, responses to this constitution introduced a "period of liturgical euphoria."[16] Altars—against the wall for at least the last thousand years—were moved into the middle of the room, and the priest celebrated the Eucharist facing the people instead of with his back to them. (One liturgical scholar said that his Wesleyan grandmother had previously believed "the priest had a crab on the altar and all his fiddling around with his back to the people was to prevent the crab from crawling off!")[17] Minor side altars and the private devotions that had been performed there disappeared. Centuries of devotional art was removed. New churches were frequently built in a circular pattern to increase the sense of equality between priest and people, and they contained very little adornment. Sundays were emphasized; saints' days and popular devotions were played down. Priests wore simpler vestments; nuns ceased to wear distinctive habits. The ancient practice of extensive training for converts was revived by the new RCIA (Rite of Christian Initiation of Adults) curriculum. The guitar music of popular culture seemed to invade the church overnight, with folk masses multiplying and youth catered to: "At some Newman Centers [college Catholic fellowships], it was found that the best time for Mass was Friday night after dates. Everyone tried banners and balloons."[18] Women were allowed to read Scripture, pray in public, usher, and serve as altar girls and church musicians.

And that was only the beginning.

THE CHURCH IN THE WORLD

The two constitutions on the church, *Lumen Gentium* and *Gaudium et Spes*, were equally transformative. *Lumen Gentium* continued to maintain what Tridentine Catholicism had always maintained—that the Catholic Church was the fullest expression of the Christian faith on earth, and that it was properly constituted under the pope and its bishops. Yet it looked at many of these things in a new way, especially when relating to non-Catholic Christians. After describing how Christ had established the church as his body, "which in the Creed is professed as one, holy, catholic and apostolic, which our Savior, after His Resurrection, commissioned Peter to shepherd," the document added:

> This Church constituted and organized in the world as a
> society, subsists in the Catholic Church, which is governed
> by the successor of Peter and by the Bishops in communion

with him, although many elements of sanctification and of truth are found outside of its visible structure.[19]

The phrase "subsist in" (*subsistit in*) drew criticism from many Catholics then and later; it seemed to contradict the church's long-standing, oft-stated principle that the body of Christ *was* the Catholic Church.[20] Later in the document, non-Catholics were referred to several times as "separated brethren"—which may not seem like much until you realize that use of this term had been urged in place of calling other Christians heretics. The overall impression from *Lumen gentium* is that, while the fullness of the church dwells in Catholicism, Christ can and does dwell elsewhere, and salvation is obtainable wherever Christ dwells.

Furthermore, in another declaration from the council, *Nostra Aetate*, the church revised its approach to Judaism, Islam, Hinduism, and Buddhism. In the aftermath of the horrors of the Holocaust, the church rejected anti-Semitism and any blame leveled at Jews for the death of Christ, and it called for dialogue with other faiths:

> The Catholic Church rejects nothing that is true and holy in these religions. She regards with sincere reverence those ways of conduct and of life, those precepts and teachings which, though different in many aspects from the ones she holds and sets forth, nonetheless often reflect a ray of that Truth which enlightens all men.[21]

Lumen gentium also represented a swing away from the focus on church hierarchy and the glorification of religious life. It exalted the role of Catholic laity, devoting an entire chapter to their existence and mission and reminding them of their importance in the work of the church:

The laity are gathered together in the People of God and make up the Body of Christ under one head. Whoever they are they are called upon, as living members, to expend all their energy for the growth of the Church and its continuous sanctification, since this very energy is a gift of the Creator and a blessing of the Redeemer.[22]

It also emphasized the collegial relationship of bishops with each other and their role in advising the pope.

Gaudium et Spes (composed in large part by *nouvelle* theologian Chenu) was one of the last documents to arise from the council—and it is from *Gaudium et Spes* that the quote comes with which this chapter began, making it clear that the church was not only speaking for Catholics and to Catholics.[23] Thoroughly explaining the problems of the modern world, it dwelt particularly on marriage and the family, economic and social problems, political unrest, and the need for peace. While it recommended the orthodox Christian gospel in response, it also emphasized the necessity for cooperation and listening:

Respect and love ought to be extended also to those who think or act differently than we do in social, political and even religious matters. In fact, the more deeply we come to understand their ways of thinking through such courtesy and love, the more easily will we be able to enter into dialogue with them.[24]

It also continued to urge the role and responsibility of Christians, especially lay Christians, in the world:

This council exhorts Christians, as citizens of two cities, to strive to discharge their earthly duties conscientiously and in response to the Gospel spirit. They are mistaken who, knowing that we have here no abiding city but seek one which is to come, think that they may therefore shirk their earthly responsibilities.[25]

The window was open, and the fresh air had been let in.

THE ROAD FROM THE COUNCIL

Both its approvers and its detractors came to view Vatican II as a reversal, not only of Vatican I and other attempts to shore up the power of the church, but ultimately of Trent. Some wanted the council to go further than it did; when the church affirmed that priestly celibacy would continue in *Sacerdotalis Caelibatus* (1967), and reiterated the long-standing opposition to artificial birth control in *Humanae Vitae* (1968), many priests and lay-people left—either becoming Protestant or leaving Christianity entirely. For a brief moment, it had seemed as though everything was possible. Everything was not. But some new things were.

The council led to greater ecumenical and interfaith in-volvement on the part of Catholics. They became active ob-servers of the WCC, acknowledging "that it is the Holy Spirit who has inspired contemporary efforts to arrive at greater Christian unity."[26] Church leaders called for a new emphasis on missions, too, both to those who had never heard the gospel and to those who had fallen away from practicing the faith. Paul VI named this the "new evangelization," and John Paul II and Benedict XVI continued to popularize the term and expand on the concept.[27]

The church also established dialogues with other Christian groups—Orthodox, Anglicans, Lutherans, and Reformed in 1965, Methodists in 1966, Southern Baptists in 1971, Oriental Orthodox in 1978, and various evangelical groups in 2003 (a number of evangelicals and Catholics had also cooperated un-officially in the "Evangelicals and Catholics Together" movement from 1994 on).[28] In 1999, Catholic and Lutheran representatives agreed to a "Joint Declaration on the Doctrine of Justification," which formally revoked the condemnations each side had applied to the other in the sixteenth century.[29] Formal dialogues were also opened with representatives of Jewish, Muslim, Sikh, Hindu, and Buddhist groups.

This ecumenical outreach, coupled with a new attention in both Protestant and Catholic liturgical scholarship to the resources of the early church, began to transform the worship practices of Protestant denominations as well. In the next few decades, nearly every Protestant mainline denomination underwent a significant revision of their liturgical texts and practices on principles articulated by Vatican II and the decrees on liturgical implementation that followed. (In some cases, such revisions were guided by scholars who had served as Protestant observers at the council.) Several more decades brought a number of these changes into many evangelical and nondenominational churches. They included more congregational participation in the liturgy, expanded Scripture readings, a renewed focus on baptism and Holy Communion and on the flow of the church year, eucharistic prayers modeled on early church practices, and use of local and non-Western music and culture.[30] And yes, sometimes banners and balloons.

Not everyone agreed with the liturgical and ecumenical euphoria. Within Catholicism, a group that rejected the decisions of the council as heretical and refused to worship according to the *Novus Ordo* Mass in either Latin or the vernacular came to be known as *sedevacantists*: they argued that Vatican II had proclaimed the heresy of Modernism, and thus there had been no true pope since Pius XII died and so the "seat" of Peter was vacant (*sede vacante* in Latin). Many began to establish their own branches of Catholicism, and some even elected their own popes. Other critics stayed within Roman Catholicism but protested by forming traditionalist societies and religious orders that celebrated the Tridentine Mass in Latin. They particularly appreciated the papacy of Benedict XVI, who had been known as a conservative and had headed the Sacred Congregation for the Doctrine of the Faith before being elected pope, and they protested the ecumenical and ecological endeavors of his successor, Francis, particularly criticizing him for his support of some elements of liberation theology.

Among Protestant detractors, some simply ignored the council; others continued to protest against Catholicism just as they had since 1517. As the 1970s faded, the experiments with guitars and folk music and banners and balloons took off in two different directions. One set of liturgical reformers began to explore more deeply the use of formal liturgy and deliberate ritual and sacramental action while another set, drawing on practices that ran through the Jesus People's Christian rock all the way back to eighteenth-century revivalism, developed "contemporary" worship—bands playing modern music and star preachers delivering practical, everyday sermons.[31]

But whether loved or hated, Vatican II's impact remains present. One Protestant pastor reflected in 2019 about the way it had changed his own local context:

> For five centuries Catholic and Protestant Christians have each defined themselves partly by *not* being the other. To belong to the Church of Rome was to be on the fast lane to the place where horned people carry three-pronged spears, Protestants thought; vice-versa from Rome's perspective. At some point that stopped being true. . . .
>
> One multisite megachurch in Vancouver celebrates Communion weekly in several locations. Others practice

centering prayer or *lectio divina* (a Benedictine practice of reading and meditating on Scripture), or host Renovaré events. Few are accused of doing something "bad." They're not even accused of being not-evangelical.[32]

To Love More and Serve Better

It's been years now since two thousand clergy in Rome reached halfway across the globe into a small Methodist congregation in northern Indiana—though they did not know they were doing so, and I did not fully realize what they had done at the time. In his speech that concluded the council, Paul VI summarized its accomplishments and expressed how great the needs were that still ought to be addressed. He hoped that, through the love of humans for each other and for God, that work could begin:

> This is our hope at the conclusion of this Second Vatican Ecumenical Council and at the beginning of the human and religious renewal which the council proposed to study and promote; this is our hope for you, brothers and Fathers of the council; this is our hope for the whole of mankind which here we have learned to love more and to serve better.[33]

The work has been nowhere near as easy or as quick as he hoped. But the meeting he was concluding had profoundly altered the terms under which it was, and is, undertaken.

Recommended Reading

Aulén, Gustaf. *Christus Victor*. New York: Macmillan, 1931.

Boersma, Hans. *Nouvelle Théologie and Sacramental Ontology: A Return to Mystery*. Oxford: Oxford University Press, 2009.

Carey, Patrick. *American Catholic Religious Thought*. New York: Paulist, 1983.

Dix, Gregory. *The Shape of the Liturgy*. London: Dacre, 1945.

Lamb, Matthew L., and Matthew Levering, eds. *The Reception of Vatican II*. Oxford: Oxford University Press, 2017.

O'Malley, John. *What Happened at Vatican II?* Cambridge, MA: Harvard University Press, 2010.

Stookey, Lawrence Hull. *Baptism: Christ's Act in the Church*. Nashville: Abingdon, 1982.

———. *Calendar: Christ's Time for the Church*. Nashville: Abingdon, 1996.

———. *Eucharist: Christ's Feast with the Church*. Nashville: Abingdon, 1993.

White, James F. *Christian Worship in Transition*. Nashville: Abingdon, 1976.

———. *New Forms of Worship*. Nashville: Abingdon, 1971.

———. *Roman Catholic Worship: Trent to Today*. Mahwah, NJ: Paulist, 1995.

CONCLUSION

Now you have a road map in your hands. It presents most of the major interstates and thoroughfares through the history of the Christian church. And the side roads and exits have been sketched out and signposted well enough, I hope, that if you choose, you may turn down one or another and explore the countryside that you find there.

We've looked at the major bend in the road caused by Christianity's legalization; we've seen the paths not taken that would have led away from the church affirming Christ as truly human and truly divine; we've witnessed the two major places where the roads forked, first separating Eastern and Western Christianity and then separating Western Christians from each other; and we've concluded by noting several spots along the way where believers have tried to reroute those diverging roads so that they once again meet, or at least run parallel to each other. And, of course, this map is still being drawn, with new streets added and landmasses discovered every day as the church continues to grow, change, and seek to follow Christ every day.

All along the way my hope has been that this map gives you more than the names and dates necessary to follow the road. In conjunction with other books in this series and with the resources recommended in the endnotes, I hope that it introduces you to sources you can consult to find guidance along the way—tour guides and guidebooks, if I'm not pushing my metaphor too far—in the words and actions of believers from the past. They too are brothers and sisters in Christ, mothers and fathers in faith. They too have things to tell us. Sometimes their words and actions may inspire us to follow in their footsteps. Sometimes they may inspire us to turn down a different road.

One of my favorite authors, G. K. Chesterton, once wrote in one of my favorite books, *Orthodoxy*, "Tradition means giving a vote to the most obscure of all classes, our ancestors. It is the democracy of the dead. Tradition refuses to submit to the small and arrogant oligarchy [rule] of those who merely happen to be walking about."[1] Chesterton meant that quote first of all in a political context; but as I read on when I first encountered his book as a young Christian, it became clear that he intended it to have religious implications as well. Reading those words was part of what started me on my path to becoming a church historian. I had listened, I realized, too much to the voices of my own day and not enough to the voices of my ancestors as I sought to understand what the Bible said and to know what was good to do as a follower of Christ.

So I have been challenged again as I sketched this map for you, challenged by Christ's desire that his church be one (Jn 17:21), holy (Mt 5:48), catholic (Mt 28:19), and apostolic (Lk 24:47)—and challenged by its frequent failure, throughout the ages, to live up to the mission he gave us.

But I am also encouraged as I look at the map that it does, as a matter of fact, show a clear road for us to follow through the last two thousand years. Many scholars believe that the description of Jesus' humility in Philippians 2 is in fact a very ancient hymn sung by the earliest believers. Read it closely in light of our journey together through the last seven chapters:

[Christ Jesus], though he was in the form of God,
    did not regard equality with God
    as something to be exploited,
but emptied himself,
    taking the form of a slave,
    being born in human likeness.
And being found in human form,
    he humbled himself
    and became obedient to the point of death—
    even death on a cross.

Therefore God also highly exalted him
    and gave him the name
    that is above every name,
so that at the name of Jesus
    every knee should bend,
    in heaven and on earth and under the earth,
and every tongue should confess
    that Jesus Christ is Lord,
    to the glory of God the Father. (Phil 2:6-11)

That is recognizably still the faith borne through all the conflicts, struggles, wars, intrigues, debates, divisions, and problems of the last two thousand years. It is recognizably still the faith that arose victorious as countless heresies were left behind on the road as dead ends. It is recognizably still the faith that Christians confess today. That fact gives me all kinds of hope and reminds me that I serve a God of grace. It reminded Chesterton of that, too. I think I may let him have the last word:

It is easy to be a madman: it is easy to be a heretic. It is always easy to let the age have its head; the difficult thing is to keep one's own. It is always easy to be a modernist; as it is easy to be a snob. To have fallen into any of those open traps of error and exaggeration which fashion after fashion and sect after sect set along the historic path of Christendom—that would indeed have been simple. . . . But to have avoided them all has been one whirling adventure; and in my vision the heavenly chariot flies thundering through the ages, the dull heresies sprawling and prostrate, the wild truth reeling but erect.[2]

NOTES

INTRODUCTION

[1]A wonderful new and accessible book that approaches the study of history in general as a conversation between us and the past is Robert Tracy McKenzie, *A Little Book for New Historians* (Downers Grove, IL: InterVarsity Press, 2019).

1 THE EDICT OF MILAN (313)

[1]You can begin to unpack what it was like in the early church through Peter Brown, *The World of Late Antiquity* (New York: Norton, 1971); Elizabeth Clark, *Women in the Early Church* (Wilmington, DE: Glazier, 1983); James S. Jeffers, *Conflict at Rome* (Minneapolis: Fortress, 1991); Ralph Martin Novak, *Christianity and the Roman Empire* (Harrisburg, PA: Trinity Press, 1991); Michael Grant, *A Social History of Greece and Rome* (New York: Scribner, 1992); Florence Dupont, *Daily Life in Ancient Rome* (Oxford: Blackwell, 2008); and James Papandrea, *A Week in the Life of Rome* (Downers Grove, IL: InterVarsity Press, 2019). Also see *Christian History* 27 (1990) on persecution in the early church; *Christian History* 37 (1993) on worship in the early church; *Christian History* 105 (2013) on early African Christianity; and *Christian History* 124 (2017) on early Christianity as an urban faith.

[2]Paul Halsall, ed., "Galerius and Constantine: Edicts of Toleration 311/313," *Internet History Sourcebooks Project*, Fordham University Center for Medieval Studies, last modified January 2, 2020, https://sourcebooks .fordham.edu/source/edict-milan.asp.

[3]Martin Marty, *A Short History of Christianity* (Philadelphia: Fortress, 1959), 41-50. See also N. T. Wright, *Paul: A Biography* (New York: HarperOne,

2018); and Paula Frederikson, *When Christians Were Jews* (New Haven, CT: Yale University Press, 2019).

4"The Tumultuous Life of Early Urban Christianity," *Christian History* 124 (2017): 22.

5Joel C. Elowsky, "Life in the Earthly City," *Christian History* 124 (2017): 6.

6Bradley P. Nystrom and David P. Nystrom, *The History of Christianity: An Introduction* (Boston: McGraw-Hill, 2004), 57.

7Gary B. Ferngren, "Healing the City," *Christian History* 124 (2017): 17.

8Nystrom and Nystrom, *History of Christianity*, 57.

9Nystrom and Nystrom, *History of Christianity*, 58.

10*Apologeticum* (*Apology*), The Tertullian Project, accessed September 4, 2020, www.tertullian.org/works/apologeticum.htm.

11"From the Archives: Nero's Cruelties," *Christian History* 27 (1990): 7.

12Paul L. Maier, trans. and comm., *Eusebius: The Church History* (Grand Rapids, MI: Kregel, 2007), 75.

13Maier, *Eusebius: The Church History*, 93.

14Dwight D. Brautigam, "Christians on Trial," *Christian History* 123 (2017): 11.

15"Polycarp's Martyrdom," Christian History Institute, accessed August 23, 2018, https://christianhistoryinstitute.org/study/module/polycarp; see Roy Stults and Jennifer Woodruff Tait, "Prison as a Parish: Christian Inmates," *Christian History* 123 (2017): 6. Kenneth Berding, *The Apostolic Fathers: A Narrative Introduction* (Eugene, OR: Wipf & Stock, 2017), tells the story of Polycarp's martyrdom and also uses it to introduce the writings of many of the earliest church fathers.

16Perpetua, "Mine Was the Victory," *Christian History* 123 (2017): 14.

17William H. C. Frend, "When Christianity Triumphed," *Christian History* 27 (1990): 9.

18J. Warren Smith, "See How These Christians Love One Another," *Christian History* 105 (2013): 31.

19There is evidence that some Christians served as public officials and that quite a few served in the army. See Rex D. Butler, "The Things That Are Caesar's," *Christian History* 124 (2017): 24-28.

20Frend, "When Christianity Triumphed," 9.

21Frend, "When Christianity Triumphed," 10.

22Brautigam, "Christians on Trial," 11.

23See Willy Rordorf et al., *The Eucharist of the Early Christians*, trans. Matthew J. O'Connell (New York: Pueblo, 1978).

24"Christianity in the Cities, Did You Know?," *Christian History* 124 (2017): 1.

[25]Grant, *Social History*, 70.

[26]Peter Kirby, ed., "The Didache: The Lord's Teaching Through the Twelve Apostles to the Nations," *Early Christian Writings*, chap. 1, accessed September 4, 2020, www.earlychristianwritings.com/text/didache-roberts .html.

[27]Kirby, "Didache," chap. 8.

[28]Kirby, "Didache," chaps. 14 and 15.

[29]Kirby, "Didache," chap. 7.

[30]Justin Martyr, "How We Christians Worship," trans. and comm. Everett Ferguson, *Christian History* 37 (1993): 11.

[31]Kevin Edgecomb, ed., "The Apostolic Tradition of Hippolytus," section 14, *Biblicalia*, accessed October 17, 2020, www.bombaxo.com/hippolytus-the -apostolic-tradition/.

[32]Edgecomb, "Apostolic Tradition of Hippolytus," 41.18.

[33]For more on Constantine, see Charles Odahl, *Constantine and the Christian Empire* (London: Routledge, 2004); Paul Stephenson, *Constantine: Roman Emperor, Christian Victor* (New York: Overlook, 2007); Peter Leithart, *Defending Constantine: The End of an Empire and the Dawn of Christendom* (Downers Grove, IL: InterVarsity Press, 2010).

[34]Stephenson, *Constantine*, 2.

[35]Maier, "The Four Emperors," in *Eusebius: The Church History*, 283-85, has a nice concise summary of the Tetrarchy (as it was called) and how it operated.

[36]Maier, *Eusebius: The Church History*, 305.

[37]Odahl, *Constantine*, 105.

[38]Odahl, *Constantine*, 106.

[39]Odahl, *Constantine*, 108.

[40]Leithart, *Defending Constantine*, 299-300.

[41]Maier, *Eusebius: The Church History*, 306. The entire edict appears in Maier, *Eusebius: The Church History*, 322-24. It was actually proclaimed at Nicomedia, but over the years it became more often associated with the place of its writing.

[42]Halsall, "Galerius and Constantine."

[43]Leithart, *Defending Constantine*, 299-300.

[44]Leithart, *Defending Constantine*, 300.

2 The Nicene Creed (325)

[1]They were each allowed to bring up to two priests and three deacons with them, so the actual number of people was much higher than three hundred.

[2]Some books to look at to begin to understand Nicaea and what followed are John Behr, *The Way to Nicaea* (Crestwood, NY: St. Vladimir's Seminary Press, 2001); Rowan Williams, *Arius* (London: SCM, 2001); R. P. C. Hanson, *The Search for the Christian Doctrine of God* (Grand Rapids, MI: Baker Academic, 2005); Lewis Ayres, *Nicaea and Its Legacy* (Oxford: Oxford University Press, 2006); Steven Need, *Truly Divine and Truly Human* (London: SPCK, 2008); Frances M. Young with Andrew Teal, *From Nicaea to Chalcedon*, 2nd ed. (Grand Rapids, MI: Baker Academic, 2010); Khaled Anatolios, *Retrieving Nicaea* (Grand Rapids, MI: Baker Academic, 2011); and Timothy George, ed., *Evangelicals and Nicene Faith* (Grand Rapids, MI: Baker Academic, 2011). Also check out *Christian History* 43 (1994) on the origins of the biblical canon; *Christian History* 51 (1996) on heresy in the early church; *Christian History* 57 (1998) on evangelism in the early church; *Christian History* 80 (2003) on the church fathers and the Bible; *Christian History* 85 (2005) on the Council of Nicaea; and *Christian History* 96 (2007) on the Gnostics.

[3]D. H. Williams, "Which Creed Is Which?," *Christian History & Biography* 85 (2005): 17. This portion of the statement was removed in 381, as we'll discuss in a bit.

[4]See Kenneth Berding, *The Apostolic Fathers: A Narrative Introduction* (Eugene, OR: Wipf & Stock, 2017).

[5]Joseph T. Lienhard, "The First Battle for the Bible," *Christian History* 80 (2003): 12.

[6]Lienhard, "First Battle for the Bible," 13.

[7]John Behr, "Midwife of the Christian Bible," *Christian History* 80 (2003): 16.

[8]Behr, "Midwife of the Christian Bible," 16.

[9]D. H. Williams, "The Earliest 'Mere Christianity,'" *Christian History and Biography* 96 (2007): 25.

[10]Williams, "Earliest 'Mere Christianity,'" 25.

[11]John Anthony McGuckin, "The Road to Nicaea," *Christian History & Biography* 85 (2005): 18-19.

[12]Elesha Coffman, "Saints and Heretics," *Christian History & Biography* 85 (2005): 31.

[13]Coffman, "Saints and Heretics," 31.

[14]McGuckin, "Road to Nicaea," 21.

[15]Bruce Shelley, "The Emperor's New Religion," *Christian History* 57 (1998): 40.

[16]Robert Payne, "A Hammer Struck at Heresy," *Christian History* 51 (1996): 17.

[17]Paul L. Maier, "Taking Care of (Church) Business," *Christian History & Biography* 85 (2005): 24.

[18]Maier, "Taking Care of (Church) Business," 24. Later, the Western church *would* enforce celibacy, and it would become one of the defining issues in conflict between West and East.

[19]Maier, "Taking Care of (Church) Business," 24.

[20]McGuckin, "Road to Nicaea," 22.

[21]McGuckin, "Road to Nicaea," 23.

[22]Payne, "Hammer Struck at Heresy," 19.

[23]Christopher A. Hall, "How Arianism Almost Won," *Christian History & Biography* 85 (2005): 36.

[24]Lewis Ayres, "The Final Act," *Christian History & Biography* 85 (2005): 39.

[25]"Sifting Through the Christ Controversies," *Christian History* 51 (2006): 20-21.

[26]Patrick Henry Reardon, "Athanasius: Pugnacious Defender of Orthodoxy," *Christian History & Biography* 85 (2005): 33.

[27]Athanasius, *On the Incarnation of the Word*, 8.54, Christian Classics Ethereal Library, accessed September 7, 2020, www.ccel.org/ccel/athanasius /incarnation.ix.html.

[28]Payne, "Hammer Struck at Heresy," 18.

[29]Bruce L. Shelley, "Fine-Tuning the Incarnation," *Christian History* 51 (1996): 24.

[30]Shelley, "Fine-Tuning the Incarnation," 24.

[31]"The Defining Moment," *Christian History* 51 (1996): 25.

[32]"The Defining Moment," 25.

[33]Dan Brown, *The Da Vinci Code* (New York: Doubleday, 2003).

3 *THE RULE OF SAINT BENEDICT* (C. 530)

[1]The translation used is from *Saint Benedict's Rule for Monasteries*, trans. Leonard J. Doyle (Collegeville, MN: Liturgical Press, 2001), chap. 1, accessed online at *The Rule of Saint Benedict: English*, Order of St. Benedict, May 6, 2006, http://archive.osb.org/rb/text/rbejms1.html. This site contains the entire *Rule*, arranged in daily readings. For a pocket paperback

edition, see Saint Benedict, *RB 1980: The Rule of St. Benedict in English*, trans. Timothy Fry (Collegeville, MN: Liturgical Press, 1981); for scholarly editions, see Saint Benedict, *RB 1980: The Rule of St. Benedict in Latin and English with Notes*, trans. and ed. Timothy Fry (Collegeville, MN: Liturgical Press, 1981), and Terrence G. Kardong, *Benedict's Rule: A Translation and Commentary* (Collegeville, MN: Liturgical Press, 1996). One of the best daily devotional books for reading through the *Rule* is Joan Chittister, *The Radical Christian Life: A Year with Saint Benedict* (Collegeville, MN: Liturgical Press, 2011); also check out Chittister's *The Rule of Benedict: Insights for the Ages* (New York: Crossroad, 1996). For the history of monasticism in general, look at *Christian History* 60 (1998) on Celtic religion, *Christian History* 64 (1999) on the desert fathers, *Christian History and Biography* 93 (2007) on Benedict and Western monasticism, and *Christian History* 108 (2014) on Charlemagne and his times.

[2]Carmen Acevedo Butcher, "The Blessing of Benedict," *Christian History & Biography* 93 (2007): 10-15.

[3]Home page, New Mellaray Abbey, accessed September 22, 2020, https://newmelleray.org/.

[4]Columba Stewart, *Prayer and Community: The Benedictine Tradition* (Maryknoll, NY: Orbis Books, 1998), 17.

[5]Saint Benedict, *RB 1980*, 27.

[6]See Anna M. Silvas, trans. and ed., *The Rule of St. Basil in Latin and English* (Collegeville, MN: Liturgical Press, 2013).

[7]Jennifer Hevelone-Harper, "Radical Christians," *Christian History and Biography* 93 (2007): 8.

[8]Saint Benedict, *RB 1980*, 51.

[9]Saint Benedict, *RB 1980*, 52. Ironically, Martin's feast day (November 11) is Remembrance Day in the United Kingdom and Veterans' Day in the United States since it was the day when World War I ended!

[10]Hevelone-Harper, "Radical Christians," 9.

[11]Vincent of Lérins, "A General Rule for Distinguishing the Truth of the Catholic Faith from the Falsehood of Heretical Pravity," *Commonitorium* 2.6, in the *Nicene and Post-Nicene Fathers*, accessed September 8, 2020, www.ccel.org/ccel/schaff/npnf211.iii.iii.html. In Latin the phrase is *teneatur quod ubique, quod semper, quod ab omnibus creditum est.*

[12]Fry, *RB 1980*, 60.

[13]Fry, *RB 1980*, 64.

[14]An excellent timeline of Benedict's life can be found in Carmen Acevedo Butcher, *Man of Blessing: A Life of St. Benedict* (Brewster, MA: Paraclete Press, 2006), 13-18. *Man of Blessing* essentially retells Pope Gregory's *Life* in modern language.

[15]Pope Gregory the Great, "How Holy Benedict Wrote a Rule for His Monks," in *Dialogues: Life of Saint Benedict*, bk. 2, chap. 36, Order of St. Benedict, July 25, 2001, www.osb.org/gen/greg/dia-38.html#P208_90533.

[16]Pope Gregory the Great, "Prologue," in *Dialogues: Life of Saint Benedict*, bk. 2, July 25, 2001, Order of St. Benedict, www.osb.org/gen/greg/dia-02 .html#P27_979.

[17]Gregory the Great, "Of a Miracle Wrought by His Sister, Scholastica," in *Dialogues: Life of Benedict*, bk. 2, chap. 33, Order of St. Benedict, revised May 16, 2018, www.osb.org/gen/scholastica.html.

[18]Butcher, *Man of Blessing*, 34.

[19]Butcher, *Man of Blessing*, 45.

[20]The term *abbot*, long in use for the head of a monastery, derives from the Aramaic title *abba*, "father," given to many of the desert fathers.

[21]Saint Benedict, "Prologue," *Rule of Saint Benedict: English*, www.archive .osb.org/rb/text/rbejms1.html#pro.

[22]Stewart, *Prayer and Community*, 21.

[23]"What Are the Instruments of Good Works," in *Rule of Benedict: English*, chap. 4, www.archive.osb.org/rb/text/rbejms2.html#4.

[24]Hugh Feiss, "A Life of Listening," *Christian History & Biography* 93 (2007): 17.

[25]"On the Reception of Guests," in *Rule of Benedict: English*, chap. 53, www .archive.osb.org/rb/text/rbeaad1.html#53.

[26]"On the Measure of Drink," in *Rule of Benedict: English*, chap. 40, www .archive.osb.org/rb/text/rbemjo2.html#40.

[27]Saint Benedict, *RB 1980*, 161.

[28]Gregory the Great, "How Venerable Benedict Did Prophesy to His Monks the Time of His Own Death," in *Dialogues: Life of Saint Benedict*, bk. 2, chap. 37, Order of St. Benedict, July 25, 2001, www.osb.org/gen/greg/dia -39.html#P211_91273.

[29]Stephanus Hilpisch, *Benedictinism Through Changing Centuries*, trans. Leonard Doyle (Collegeville, MN: St. John's Abbey, 1958), 19.

[30]Anselm is also responsible for the famous statement "I do not seek to understand in order that I may believe, but rather, I believe in order that I may understand" from his *Proslogion*, which he based on a concept he

found in Augustine. Anselm, *Proslogion,* section 1, accessed September 8, 2020, www.thelatinlibrary.com/anselmproslogion.html.

[31]Hilpisch, *Benedictinism,* 23.

[32]Saint Benedict, *RB 1980,* 121. See also G. R. Evans, *The I. B. Tauris History of Monasticism: The Western Tradition* (London: Tauris, 2016), 94.

[33]Sarah Morice Brubaker, "The Idea of Christendom," *Christian History* 108 (2014): 21.

[34]Saint Benedict, *RB 1980,* 121.

[35]Saint Benedict, *RB 1980,* 123.

[36]Saint Benedict, *RB 1980,* 126.

[37]Evans, *I. B. Tauris History of Monasticism,* 154.

[38]Hilpisch, *Benedictinism,* 74; and Saint Benedict, *RB 1980,* 132.

[39]Evans, *I. B. Tauris History of Monasticism,* 95. Benedictines often distinguish between the "black" monks and the "white" in conversation because the Cistercians wear a white habit.

[40]Hilpisch, *Benedictinism,* 77.

[41]Evans, *I. B. Tauris History of Monasticism,* 149.

[42]Evans, *I. B. Tauris History of Monasticism,* 161.

[43]Evans, *I. B. Tauris History of Monasticism,* 162.

[44]Garry J. Crites, "Intellect That Illuminates Christian Truth," *Christian History* 116 (2015): 17.

[45]Evans, *I. B. Tauris History of Monasticism,* 147.

[46]Evans, *I. B. Tauris History of Monasticism,* 171.

[47]See *Christian History* 127 (2018) on medieval lay mystics for more.

[48]See Julian of Norwich, *Showings,* trans. and ed. Edmund College and James Walsh, Classics of Western Spirituality (Mahwah, NJ: Paulist Press, 1978).

[49]Edwin Woodruff Tait, "Duty and Delight," *Christian History* 110 (2014): 19. For more about medieval Christianity, consult Gerd Tellenbach, *The Church in Western Europe from the Tenth to the Early Twelfth Century* (Cambridge: Cambridge University Press, 1993); Adriaan H. Bredero, *Christendom and Christianity in the Middle Ages,* trans. Reinder Bruinsma (Grand Rapids, MI: Eerdmans, 1994); Thomas F. X. Noble and Julie M. H. Smith, eds., *Early and Medieval Christianities: c. 600–c. 1100,* vol. 3 of *The Cambridge History of Christianity* (Cambridge: Cambridge University Press, 2008); and Miri Rubin and Walter Simons, eds., *Christianity in Western Europe c. 1100–c. 1500,* vol. 4 of *The Cambridge History of Christianity* (Cambridge: Cambridge University Press, 2009). Also

check out *Christian History* 30 (1991) on women in the medieval church and *Christian History* 49 (1996) on everyday life in the Middle Ages.

[50]Council of Trent, "On Regulars and Nuns," 25th Session, Seventh Decree, chap. 1, St. Gemma Web Productions, accessed September 9, 2020, www .thecounciloftrent.com/ch25.htm. "Regular" meant someone who lived under a rule, *regula*, whether Benedict's or another.

[51]One of the first Anglican religious orders was the Community of St Mary the Virgin at Wantage in England. C. S. Lewis, good friends with one of their number, dedicated *Perelandra* to "some ladies at Wantage"—a phrase erroneously, but humorously, rendered by one translator as "to some wanton ladies."

[52]The name derives from a 1998 book by Jonathan R. Wilson, *Living Faithfully in a Fragmented World*, 2nd ed. (Eugene, OR: Cascade Books, 2010). For more, see Rob Moll, "The New Monasticism," *Christianity Today*, September 2, 2005, www.christianitytoday.com/ct/2005/september/16.38 .html.

[53]Thomas Merton, *The Seven Storey Mountain* (New York: Harcourt, 1948); Kathleen Norris, *The Cloister Walk* (New York: Riverhead, 1996); Dallas Willard, *The Spirit of the Disciplines: Understanding How God Changes Lives* (New York: HarperCollins, 1998); Richard Foster, *Celebration of Discipline: The Path to Spiritual Growth* (New York: Joanna Cotler Books, 1978); and Rod Dreher, *The Benedict Option: A Strategy for Christians in a Post-Christian Nation* (New York: Sentinel, 2017).

4 THE EXCOMMUNICATION OF PATRIARCH KERULARIOS BY POPE LEO IX VIA CARDINAL HUMBERT (1054)

[1]Mark Galli, "The Great Divorce," *Christian History* 54 (1997): 10, following the account in Timothy (Kallistos) Ware, *The Orthodox Church* (Baltimore: Penguin, 1963), 51. Galli's article is basically a paraphrase of Ware's third chapter, and I have used it because of its much greater concision, but I encourage you to read Ware's fuller account. For decades it has been the most accessible book introducing Orthodoxy to Westerners. John Meyendorff's *Byzantine Theology*, 1st ed. (New York: Fordham University Press, 1974) is a deeper study of Eastern theology. Steven Runciman, *The Eastern Schism* (Oxford: Clarendon, 1955), is an accessible introduction to the schism in more detail. Also see Michael Angold, ed., *Eastern Christianity*, vol. 5 of *The Cambridge History of Christianity* (Cambridge: Cambridge University Press, 2014); and *Christian History*

44 (1994) on John Chrysostom and *Christian History* 54 (1997) on Eastern Orthodox Christianity.

[2]*Pascha* is the Greek term related to the Jewish feast of Passover. It is the word from which English speakers, via Latin, get the term "paschal Lamb," which is the lamb sacrificed at Passover. In addition, "paschal Lamb" is often used by Christians as a term for Christ.

[3]Ware, *Orthodox Church*, 308-9.

[4]Galli, "Great Divorce," 11.

[5]Ware, *Orthodox Church*, 53-54.

[6]Ware, *Orthodox Church*, 55.

[7]Meyendorff, *Byzantine Theology*, 97-100.

[8]Galli, "Great Divorce," 14.

[9]Galli, "Great Divorce," 12-13, following Ware, *Orthodox Church*, 55-56. For more, see John Meyendorff, *Rome, Constantinople, Moscow: Historical and Theological Studies* (Crestwood, NY: St. Vladimir's Seminary Press, 1996).

[10]Ware, *Orthodox Church*, 26-27.

[11]Edwin Woodruff Tait and Chris Armstrong, "Three Wise Men from the East," *Christian History* 80 (2003): 35; and Robert A. Krupp, "Golden Tongue and Iron Will," *Christian History* 44 (1994): 7.

[12]John Chrysostom, "The Paschal Sermon," Orthodox Church in America, accessed September 9, 2020, www.oca.org/fs/sermons/the-paschal -sermon.

[13]Paul Meyendorff, "A Taste of Glory," *Christian History* 54 (1997): 41. Also see John Meyendorff, *Byzantine Theology*, 115-25.

[14]Paul Meyendorff, "Taste of Glory," 41.

[15]Bradley Nassif, "Kissers and Smashers," in "Eastern Orthodoxy: Then and Now," special issue, *Christian History* 54 (1997): 20.

[16]Nassif, "Kissers and Smashers," 21.

[17]Nassif, "Kissers and Smashers," 23. See John of Damascus, *First Apology Against Those Who Attack the Divine Images*, section 16, trans. David Anderson (Crestwood, NY: St. Vladimir's Seminary Press, 1980), as revised by Míceál F. Vaughan, 1996, http://faculty.washington.edu/miceal /Courses/CompLit280/John_of_Damascus.html.

[18]Nassif, "Kissers and Smashers," 21.

[19]Nassif, "Kissers and Smashers," 21. This event is still celebrated by the Orthodox every first Sunday of Lent and called the Feast of the Triumph of Orthodoxy.

[20]Christopher Fee, "Sacred Kingship," *Christian History* 108 (2014): 16. For more on Charlemagne and the Western Roman Empire, see Alessandro Barbero's *Charlemagne: Father of a Continent* (Berkeley: University of California Press, 2018); and Janet Nelson, *King and Emperor* (Berkeley: University of California Press, 2019).

[21]After ruling as either regent for or co-ruler with her son since 780, she had ordered him to be tortured so severely that he died in 797.

[22]Ware, *Orthodox Church*, 53.

[23]Galli, "Great Divorce," 13.

[24]Galli, "Great Divorce," 14.

[25]Meyendorff, *Byzantine Theology*, 91-94.

[26]Ware, *Orthodox Church*, 59.

[27]Ware, *Orthodox Church*, 59.

[28]Ware, *Orthodox Church*, 64.

[29]Ware, *Orthodox Church*, 65. Some scholars think the pope's name may have been removed simply as a continued protest over the *filioque* issue rather than in response to a specific letter.

[30]Ware, *Orthodox Church*, 67.

[31]Ware, *Orthodox Church*, 67.

[32]For more on the growth of the monarchical papacy and the conflicts it caused, see Colin Morris, *The Papal Monarchy: The Western Church from 1050 to 1250* (Oxford: Clarendon, 1989); I. S. Robinson, *The Papacy 1073–1198* (Cambridge: Cambridge University Press, 1990); and Aristeides Papadakis and John Meyendorff, *The Christian East and the Rise of the Papacy: The Church AD 1071–1453* (Crestwood, NY: St. Vladimir's Seminary Press, 1993).

[33]"Urban's Letter to the Faithful in Flanders, December 1095," in Edward Peters, ed., *The First Crusade: "The Chronicle of Fulcher of Chartres" and Other Source Materials* (Philadelphia: University of Pennsylvania Press, 2011), 42.

[34]Christopher Tyerman's *The World of the Crusades* (New Haven, CT: Yale University Press, 2019), is a good introduction to the Crusades.

[35]Ware, *Orthodox Church*, 68.

[36]Ware, *Orthodox Church*, 68.

[37]Ware, *Orthodox Church*, 69.

[38]Ware, *Orthodox Church*, 69.

[39]Paul Halsall, ed., "Medieval History Sourcebook: Pope Innocent III; Reprimand of Papal Legate," *Internet History Sourcebooks Project*, Fordham

University, rev. January 2, 2020, https://sourcebooks.fordham.edu/source
/1204innocent.asp.

[40]Runciman, *Eastern Schism*, 101.

[41]Mark Galli, "Better the Infidel," *Christian History* 54 (1997): 19.

[42]Ware, *Orthodox Church*, 83.

[43]Ware, *Orthodox Church*, 86.

[44]A brief introduction to modern Orthodox thought since the eighteenth
century is in Andrew Louth, *Modern Orthodox Thinkers* (Downers
Grove, IL: InterVarsity Press, 2015).

[45]"Joint Catholic-Orthodox Declaration of His Holiness Pope Paul VI and
the Ecumenical Patriarch Athenagoras I," 4.B and 5, December 7, 1965,
w2.vatican.va/content/paul-vi/en/speeches/1965/documents/hf_p-vi
_spe_19651207_common-declaration.html.

5 Martin Luther's *Ninety-Five Theses* (1517)

[1]There are a *lot* of books about the Reformation. You might start with
James Payton, *Getting the Reformation Wrong* (Downers Grove, IL: Inter-
Varsity Press, 2010). Diarmaid MacCulloch's *Reformation: A History*
(New York: Penguin, 2003) is massive and complete; shorter introduc-
tions include Lewis Spitz, *The Protestant Reformation, 1517–1559* (Saint
Louis, MO: Concordia, 2001); and Euan Cameron, *The European Refor-
mation* (Oxford: Oxford University Press, 2012). The classic biography
of Luther is Roland Bainton, *Here I Stand* (New York: Abingdon, 1950),
although quite a lot of scholarship has been done since then. Heiko
Obermann, *Luther: Man Between God and the Devil* (New Haven, CT:
Yale University Press, 1989), is academically rigorous but can be hard to
read. More accessible are Martin Marty, *Martin Luther* (New York:
Penguin, 2004); James Kittelson and Hans Wiersma, *Luther the Reformer*
(Minneapolis: Fortress, 2016); and David C. Steinmetz, *Luther in Context*,
2nd ed. (Grand Rapids, MI: Baker Academic, 2002). *Christian History*
did a five-issue series on the Reformation: 115 (2015) on Luther; 118 (2016)
on the Urban Reformation; 120 (2016) on Calvin; 122 (2017) on the
Catholic Reformation; and 131 (2019) on women in the sixteenth century.

[2]Eric W. Gritsch, "The Straw That Broke the Camel's Back," *Christian
History* 116 (2015): 26.

[3]Armin Siedlecki and Perry Brown, "Preachers and Printers," *Christian
History* 118 (2016): 22.

[4]Gritsch, "Straw That Broke the Camel's Back," 26.

[5]James M. Kittelson, "The Accidental Revolutionary," *Christian History* 34 (1992): 14-15.

[6]Bainton, *Here I Stand*, 103.

[7]Kittelson, "Accidental Revolutionary," 15.

[8]Kittelson and Wiersma, *Luther the Reformer*, 161. He *may* have added the phrase "Here I stand. I can do no other. God help me! Amen."

[9]Kirsi Irmeli Stjerna, *Women and the Reformation* (Malden, MA: Blackwell, 2009), 53.

[10]Mark U. Edwards Jr., "After the Revolution," *Christian History* 39 (1993): 13.

[11]Read more about Erasmus in James Tracy, *Erasmus of the Low Countries* (Berkeley: University of California Press, 1996), and read some of his works in Erika Rummel, ed., *The Erasmus Reader* (Toronto: University of Toronto Press, 1990). The most basic scholarly introductions to the Urban Reformation is Steven Ozment, *The Reformation in the Cities* (New Haven, CT: Yale University Press, 1975).

[12]David Fink, "The Man Who Yielded to No One," *Christian History* 115 (2015): 49.

[13]Fink, "Man Who Yielded to No One," 48.

[14]Rummel, *Erasmus Reader*, 195; Fink, "Man Who Yielded to No One," 49.

[15]Jim West and Edwin Woodruff Tait, "When the State Advanced the Church," *Christian History* 118 (2016): 6.

[16]West and E. Woodruff Tait, "When the State Advanced the Church," 7.

[17]You can read a bit more about them in Diane Poythress, *Reformer of Basel* (Grand Rapids, MI: Reformation Heritage Books, 2011), and D. F. Wright, *Martin Bucer* (Cambridge: Cambridge University Press, 2002), as well as in *Christian History* 131 (2019).

[18]Find out more about the Peasants' War in Peter Blickle, *The Revolution of 1525* (Baltimore: Johns Hopkins University Press, 1981).

[19]Edwin Woodruff Tait, "They Wanted God to Save His Own," *Christian History* 118 (2016): 19.

[20]Kenneth R. Bartlett and Margaret McGlynn, eds., *The Renaissance and Reformation in Northern Europe* (Toronto: University of Toronto Press, 2014), 70-71.

[21]E. Woodruff Tait, "They Wanted God to Save His Own," 20.

[22]Walter Klaassen and John Oyer, "A Fire That Spread," *Christian History* 118 (2016): 29. Read more about the Anabaptists in Walter Klaassen, *Anabaptism* (Waterloo, Ont.: Conrad Press, 1973); Arnold Snyder, *Anabaptist*

History & Theology (Kitchener, Ont.: Pandora Press, 1985); and John Oyer, *They Harry the Good People out of the Land* (Goshen, IN: Mennonite Historical Society, 2000).

[23]Klaassen and Oyer, "Fire That Spread," 29.

[24]For more on French Protestantism in general you can start with Mark Greengrass, *The French Reformation* (Oxford: Blackwell, 1991). Calvin, like Luther, has attracted many scholars. Some of the best books on him are Ronald Wallace, *Calvin, Geneva, and the Reformation* (Grand Rapids, MI: Baker Books, 1990); Richard Muller, *The Unaccommodated Calvin* (Oxford: Oxford University Press, 2002); François Wendel, *Calvin* (Grand Rapids, MI: Baker Books, 2002); Herman J. Selderhuis, *John Calvin: A Pilgrim's Life* (Downers Grove, IL: InterVarsity Press, 2009); David C. Steinmetz, *Calvin in Context*, 2nd ed. (Oxford: Oxford University Press, 2010); and Jon Balserak, *John Calvin as Sixteenth-Century Prophet* (Oxford: Oxford University Press, 2014).

[25]John Calvin, "Preface," *Commentary on the Psalms* (1557), accessed September 9, 2020, www.ccel.org/ccel/calvin/calcom08.vi.html.

[26]Olivier Fatio, "Pastor of Geneva," *Christian History* 120 (2016): 9.

[27]Good introductions to the English Reformation include A. G. Dickens, *The English Reformation* (University Park: Pennsylvania State University Press, 1991); J. J. Scarisbrick, *The Reformation and the English People* (Oxford: Blackwell, 1991); and Eamon Duffy, *The Stripping of the Altars* (New Haven, CT: Yale University Press, 2005).

[28]The confusing aspects of all of this theological seesawing on the local parish level are beautifully pictured in John Moorman, *The Anglican Spiritual Tradition* (Springfield, IL: Templegate, 1985), 1-12.

[29]David C. Steinmetz, *Reformers in the Wings*, 2nd ed. (Oxford: Oxford University Press, 2001), 45.

[30]Steinmetz, *Reformers in the Wings*, 45.

[31]John Olin's *The Catholic Reformation* (New York: Fordham University Press, 1996) and Martin Jones's *The Counter-Reformation* (Cambridge: Cambridge University Press, 1995) will introduce you to reform movements within Catholicism. John O'Malley's *Trent and All That* (Cambridge, MA: Harvard University Press, 2000) and *Trent: What Happened at the Council* (Cambridge, MA: Belknap, 2013) are accessible explanations of the Catholic Reformation and the specifics of Trent.

[32]Edwin Woodruff Tait, "Duty and Delight," *Christian History* 110 (2014): 14-19.

[33]Thomas Worcester, "A Renewed and Global Faith," *Christian History* 122 (2017): 23.

[34]Martin J. Lohrmann, "The Persistent Council," *Christian History* 122 (2017): 22.

6 THE EDINBURGH CONFERENCE (1910)

[1]Mark Galli, "Missions and Ecumenism: John R. Mott," *Christian History* 65 (2000): 37; and Keith Hunt and Gladys Hunt, *For Christ and the University: The Story of InterVarsity Christian Fellowship of the USA, 1940–1990* (Downers Grove, IL: InterVarsity Press, 1991), 40.

[2]Hunt and Hunt, *For Christ and the University*, 40.

[3]There are several biographies of Mott, although some are quite old. Written while he was still alive are Basil Joseph Mathews, *John R. Mott, World Citizen* (New York: Harper, 1934); and Galen Fisher, *John R. Mott, Architect of Cooperation and Unity* (New York: Association Press, 1952). More recent are Robert Mackie, *Layman Extraordinary: John R. Mott, 1865–1955* (New York: Association Press, 1965); and Charles Howard Hopkins, *John R. Mott: A Biography* (Grand Rapids, MI: Eerdmans, 1979). You can find many resources at "Mott, John R. (1865–1955)," School of Theology, Boston University, accessed September 11, 2020, www.bu.edu/missiology/missionary-biography/l-m/mott-john-r-1865-1955/, and at "John R. Mott," The Nobel Peace Prize 1946, *The Nobel Prize*, accessed September 11, 2020, www.nobelprize.org/prizes/peace/1946/mott/biographical/.

[4]Some books on the history of colonization and exploration include Perry Miller, *Errand into the Wilderness* (Cambridge, MA: Belknap, 1956); Richard Hofstadter, *America at 1750: A Social Portrait* (New York: Vintage Books, 1971): David Sweet and Gary Nash, eds., *Struggle & Survival in Colonial America* (Berkeley: University of California Press, 1982); Thomas Tweed, ed., *Retelling America's Religious History* (Berkeley: University of California Press, 1997); Kenneth Mills, William Taylor, and Sandra Lauderdale Graham, eds., *Colonial Latin America* (Wilmington, DE: Scholarly Resources, 2002); Brian Fagan, *Fish on Friday: Feasting, Fasting, and the Discovery of the New World* (New York: Basic Books, 2006); *Christian History* 35 (1992) on Columbus, and *Christian History* 130 (2019) on Latin American Christianity.

[5]Gary Y. Okihiro, *American History Unbound: Asians and Pacific Islanders* (Berkeley: University of California Press, 2015), 57. See also Brian Larkin, "Christianity Converted," *Christian History* 130 (2019): 6-11.

[6]Some books that will introduce you to Christian concerns in the Enlightenment include Charles Hummel, *The Galileo Connection* (Downers Grove, IL: InterVarsity Press, 1986); David Lindberg and Ronald Numbers, eds., *God and Nature: Historical Essays on the Encounter Between Christianity and Science* (Berkeley: University of California Press, 1986); and Kenneth J. Howell, *God's Two Books: Copernican Cosmology* and *Biblical Interpretation in Early Modern Science* (Notre Dame, IN: University of Notre Dame Press, 2002). For more, see *Christian History* 76 (2002) on the Christian face of the Scientific Revolution and *Christian History* 134 (2020) on Christians pursuing science in the Middle Ages and the early modern world.

[7]See Edward B. Davis, "Reading the 'Book of Nature,'" in "The Wonder of Creation," special issue, *Christian History* 119 (2016): 25-29.

[8]Paul Halsall, ed., "Modern History Sourcebook: Galileo Galilei; Letter to the Grand Duchess Christina of Tuscany, 1615," *Internet History Sourcebooks Project*, Fordham University, rev. January 21, 2020, https://sourcebooks .fordham.edu/mod/galileo-tuscany.asp.

[9]John W. O'Malley, *What Happened at Vatican II* (Cambridge, MA: Harvard University Press, 2008), 54.

[10]Edwin Gaustad, "Disciples of Reason," *Christian History* 50 (1996): 28-31. For more, see Mark Noll, *Christians in the American Revolution* (Grand Rapids, MI: Eerdmans, 1977); Harry S. Stout, *The New England Soul: Preaching and Religious Culture in Colonial New England* (Oxford: Oxford University Press, 1986); Edwin S. Gaustad, *Faith of Our Fathers: Religion and the New Nation* (New York: Harper & Row, 1987); and David Hall, *Worlds of Wonder, Days of Judgment* (Cambridge, MA: Harvard University Press, 1990).

[11]Gaustad, "Disciples of Reason," 28-29, 31.

[12]See *Christian History* 127 (2018) on medieval lay mystics, and *Christian History* 10 (1986) on Pietism, for more, as well as J. Steven O'Malley, *Early German-American Evangelicalism* (Lanham, MD: Scarecrow, 1995); Hans Schneider, *Radical Pietism* (Lanham, MD: Scarecrow, 2007); and David Shantz, *An Introduction to German Pietism* (Baltimore: Johns Hopkins University Press, 2013).

[13]For Methodism, start with Richard Heitzenrater, *Wesley and the People Called Methodists* (Nashville: Abingdon, 2013); John Wigger, *American Saint: Francis Asbury and the Methodists* (Oxford: Oxford University Press, 2009); *Christian History* 69 (2001) on the Wesleys; and *Christian*

History 114 (2015) on Francis Asbury and American Methodism. For Edwards, begin with George Marsden, *Jonathan Edwards: A Life* (New Haven, CT: Yale University Press, 2003); and *Christian History & Biography* 77 (2003). For Whitefield, read Harry S. Stout, *The Divine Dramatist: George Whitefield and the Rise of Modern Evangelicalism* (Grand Rapids, MI: Eerdmans, 1991); and *Christian History* 38 (1993).

[14]A classic book on this is Roger Finke and Rodney Stark, *The Churching of America 1776–2005* (New Brunswick, NJ: Rutgers University Press, 2005). Also see Martin E. Marty, *Pilgrims in Their Own Land: 500 Years of Religion in America* (New York: Penguin, 1984); and Peter W. Williams, *America's Religions* (Urbana: University of Illinois Press, 2008).

[15]For more on Carey, check out *Christian History* 36 (1992), along with Mary Drewery, *William Carey: A Biography* (Grand Rapids, MI: Zondervan, 1979); Timothy George, *Faithful Witness: The Life and Mission of William Carey* (Birmingham, AL: New Hope, 1999); and "Center for Study of the Life and Work of William Carey, D.D. (1761–1834)," William Carey University, accessed September 11, 2020, www.wmcarey.edu/carey/index2.html.

[16]Mark Galli, "The Man Who Wouldn't Give Up," *Christian History* 36 (1992): 11.

[17]William Carey, "The Missions Manifesto," *Christian History* 36 (1992): 18.

[18]It was soon renamed the Baptist Missionary Society and is today Baptist World Mission. For more, see Brian Stanley, *The History of the Baptist Missionary Society, 1792–1992* (Edinburgh: T&T Clark, 1992). The full title of Carey's book, by the way, was *An Enquiry into the Obligations of Christians, to Use Means for the Conversion of the Heathens in Which the Religious State of the Different Nations of the World, the Success of Former Undertakings, and the Practicability of Further Undertakings, Are Considered.*

[19]Paul Pierson, "Why Did the 1800s Explode with Missions?" *Christian History* 36 (1992): 21. There are many books on missions history in general; a few good places to start are Stephen Neill, *A History of Christian Missions* (New York: Penguin, 1994); and Ruth Tucker, *From Jerusalem to Irian Jaya: A Biographical History of Christian Missions* (Grand Rapids, MI: Eerdmans, 2004), as well as the oldie but goodie by Kenneth Scott Latourette, *A History of the Expansion of Christianity*, 7 vols. (New York: Harper & Brothers, 1937–1945). Some of the most famous missionaries from the nineteenth and early twentieth centuries

are discussed in *Christian History* 52 (1996) on Hudson Taylor and missions to China; *Christian History & Biography* 87 (2005) on Christianity in India; *Christian History & Biography* 90 (2006) on Adoniram and Ann Judson; and *Christian History* 128 (2018) on George Müller and faith missions.

[20]Pierson, "Why Did the 1800s Explode with Missions?" 21. He notes that, in 1992, when he wrote, the number of Protestant missionaries coming *to* the US from the Global South was 48,000—more than ten times the 3400 known in 1972, two decades earlier!

[21]Brian Stanley, "The World Missionary Conference, Edinburgh 1910: Sifting History from Myth," *Expository Times* 121, no. 7 (2010): 325.

[22]Thomas Askew, "The 1888 London Centenary Missions Conference: Ecumenical Disappointment or American Missions Coming of Age?" *International Bulletin of Missionary Research* 18, no. 3 (1994): 113.

[23]Stanley, "World Missionary Conference," 326.

[24]Stanley, "World Missionary Conference," 326.

[25]The 2010 conference convened to celebrate and commemorate the one in 1910 has made all these volumes available along with many other primary- and secondary-source reflections on the conference; see "Edinburgh 1910 Conference," accessed September 11, 2020, www.edinburgh2010.org /en/resources/1910-conference.html. The basic work on the conference itself is Brian Stanley, *The World Missionary Conference, Edinburgh 1910* (Grand Rapids, MI: Eerdmans, 2009).

[26]Ralph D. Winter, "The Legacy of Edinburgh, 1910," in *Foundations of the World Christian Movement: A Larger Perspective, Course Reader* (Pasadena, CA: Institute of International Studies, 2008), 300.

[27]*Report of Commission, Part I: Carrying the Gospel to All the Non-Christian World*, (Edinburgh: World Missionary Conference, 1910), 11, https://archive.org/details/reportofcommissio1worluoft/page/n11. Though Mott has become identified with the statement, the report was the work of the entire commission.

[28]*Report of Commission, Part I*, 23, https://archive.org/details/report ofcommissio1worluoft/page/23.

[29]*Report of Commission, Part II*, 107, www.archive.org/stream/reportof commissio9worluoft/page/107/.

[30]Brian Stanley, "The Church of the Three Selves: A Perspective from the World Missionary Conference, Edinburgh, 1910," *Journal of Imperial and Commonwealth History* 36, no. 3 (2008): 436; see *Report of Commission,*

Part II, 100-102, www.archive.org/stream/reportofcommissi09worluoft#page/100/.

[31]"History," Commission on World Mission and Evangelism, World Council of Churches, accessed September 11, 2020, www.oikoumene.org/en/what-we-do/cwme/history.

[32]Stanley, "World Missionary Conference," 327.

[33]Stanley, "World Missionary Conference," 327.

[34]"Commission on Faith and Order," World Council of Churches, accessed October 14, 2019, www.oikoumene.org/en/what-we-do/faith-and-order. The phrase "Faith and Order" meant that the conference was to deal with issues of both doctrine and organization. See also https://episcopalchurch.org/library/glossary/faith-and-order (accessed November 10, 2020).

[35]"Plans Mature for Universal Christian Conference," *Federal Council Bulletin* 7, no. 5 (1924): 26. There is an extensive history of the ecumenical movement in three volumes available from the WCC; the first two volumes, which discuss ecumenical efforts from 1517 to 1968, are by Ruth Rouse and Stephen O'Neill, first issued as *A History of the Ecumenical Movement, 1517-1948* (Philadelphia: Westminster Press, 1954), then reissued as *A History of the Ecumenical Movement, 1517-1968* in two volumes (Philadelphia: Westminster Press, 1967). The third volume is by John Briggs, Mercy Amba Oduyoye, and Georges Tsetsis, eds., *A History of the Ecumenical Movement, vol. 3 1968-2000* (Geneva: World Council of Churches, 2004).

[36]W. A. Visser 't Hooft published his own recollections as *The Genesis and Formation of the World Council of Churches* (Geneva: World Council of Churches, 1982). The most famous document produced by the council to date is probably *Baptism, Eucharist, and Ministry*, Faith and Order Paper no. 111, WCC (1982), www.oikoumene.org/en/resources/documents/commissions/faith-and-order/i-unity-the-church-and-its-mission/baptism-eucharist-and-ministry-faith-and-order-paper-no-111-the-lima-text.

[37]"Orthodox Churches (Eastern)," World Council of Churches, accessed September 11, 2020, www.oikoumene.org/en/church-families/orthodox-churches-eastern.

[38]The NAE founding predates the founding of the WCC but was intimately wrapped up in efforts to provide an evangelical alternative to the Federal (now National) Council of Churches, a mainline ecumenical group of US churches. For more, see "History," National Association of Evangelicals, accessed September 11, 2020, www.nae.net/about-nae/history/.

7 THE SECOND VATICAN COUNCIL (1962–1965)

[1]The Second Vatican Council is, as you will soon learn, controversial. The best short introduction is probably John O'Malley, *What Happened at Vatican II?* (Cambridge, MA: Harvard University Press, 2010). Also look at M. Basil Pennington, *The Eucharist Yesterday and Today* (New York: Crossroad, 1984); Matthew L. Lamb and Matthew Levering, eds., *Vatican II: Renewal Within Tradition* (Oxford: Oxford University Press, 2008); idem, *The Reception of Vatican II* (Oxford: Oxford University Press, 2017); and Joseph Ratzinger (now Pope Benedict XVI), *Theological Highlights of Vatican II* (Mahwah, NJ: Paulist, 2009). Some of the most famous theological and liturgical arguments that shaped the council's theology are found in Gustaf Aulén, *Christus Victor* (New York: Macmillan, 1931); Gregory Dix, *The Shape of the Liturgy* (London: Dacre, 1945); and a number of books from the *nouvelle théologie* movement explained above that are probably best introduced through the descriptions of them in Hans Boersma, *Nouvelle Théologie and Sacramental Ontology: A Return to Mystery* (Oxford: Oxford University Press, 2009). For the impact of these changes on Protestants, two books by James F. White—a key Protestant in this movement—are helpful: *New Forms of Worship* (Nashville: Abingdon, 1971) and *Christian Worship in Transition* (Nashville: Abingdon, 1976). White's *Roman Catholic Worship: Trent to Today* (Mahwah, NJ: Paulist, 1995) also deals heavily with the changes brought about by the council. *Christian History* 129 (2019), called "Recovery from Modern Amnesia," addresses these changes, especially as they affected evangelicals. While the canons of the council and some of the resulting changes in the liturgy of many denominations can be accessed online, also check out Max Thurian and Geoffrey Wainwright, eds., *Baptism and Eucharist: Ecumenical Convergence in Celebration* (Geneva: World Council of Churches, 1983).

[2]O'Malley, *What Happened at Vatican II?*, 54.

[3]The conflict between the pope and the Italian army was not settled until 1929 with the establishment of Vatican City as an independent city-state.

[4]Council Fathers, "Decrees of the First Vatican Council," 1868, Papal Encyclicals Online, last updated February 20, 2020, www.papalencyclicals .net/councils/ecum20.htm. In one sense this was an attempt to explain Pius IX's proclamation of the Immaculate Conception of Mary in 1854—the first time a pope had issued such a doctrinal definition without a council to back him up.

[5]Hans Boersma, "Going Behind Aquinas," *Christian History* 129 (2019): 28.

[6]The term *Modernism* to describe this philosophy, capitalized, dates from 1904 and the run-up to *Lamentabili* (see O'Malley, *What Happened at Vatican II?*, 69), but historians now frequently use *modernity* with a lowercase *m* to refer to general trends from the Reformation and especially the Enlightenment onwards. For more on this, especially in America, see Patrick Carey, *American Catholic Religious Thought* (New York: Paulist, 1983).

[7]Boersma, "Going Behind Aquinas," 28.

[8]O'Malley, *What Happened at Vatican II?*, 57, who adds: "This was true not only on a high theological level but also on the level of a corporate consciousness that reached down to ordinary Catholics in the pews and touched them deeply. For the first time in history, thanks to the modern media, Catholics knew the name of the reigning pope and could recognize his face."

[9]Many of these books were not translated into English until much later, or never translated, but for ease of reading I will use English translations of the titles to refer to them above. The original edition of this book is *Corpus Mysticum: Essai sur L'Eucharistie et l'Église au moyen âge* (Aubier: Paris, 1944), translated as *Corpus Mysticum: The Eucharist and the Church in the Middle Ages*, trans. Gemma Simmonds et al. (South Bend, IN: University of Notre Dame Press, 2006).

[10]*Une école de théologie: le Saulchoir* (Étiolles: Le Saulchoir, 1937) has never been translated into English.

[11]"La nouvelle théologie où va-t-elle?" *Angelicum* vol. 23, no. 3/4 (July-Dec. 1946): 126-145. The easiest English translation to access is Suzanne M. Rini, trans., "Where Is the New Theology Leading Us?", *Catholic Family News Reprint Series* #309, accessed October 19, 2020, https://archive.org /details/Garrigou-LagrangeEnglish/_Where%20is%20the%20New %20Theology%20Leading%20Us__%20-%20Garrigou-Lagrange%2C %20Reginald%2C%20O.P_/mode/2up.

[12]The official term for this, invoked frequently during the council, was *aggiornaménto*, "updating."

[13]O'Malley, *What Happened at Vatican II?*, 93.

[14]Pope Paul VI, "Constitution on the Sacred Liturgy, *Sacrosanctum Concilium*," December 4, 1963, chap. 1, II.14, www.vatican.va/archive/hist _councils/ii_vatican_council/documents/vat-ii_const_19631204 _sacrosanctum-concilium_en.html.

[15]Paul VI, "Constitution on the Sacred Liturgy," chap. 1, III.A.36.1-2.

[16]White, *Roman Catholic Worship*, 121.

[17]White, *Roman Catholic Worship*, 117.

[18]White, *Roman Catholic Worship*, 122.

[19]Pope Paul VI, "Dogmatic Constitution on the Church, *Lumen Gentium*," November 21, 1964, chap. 1, section 8, www.vatican.va/archive/hist _councils/ii_vatican_council/documents/vat-ii_const_19641121_lumen -gentium_en.html.

[20]Pope Pius XII in *Mystici Corporis Christi* (1943) had stated that the Mystical Body of Christ and the Roman Catholic Church were one and the same thing: "If we would define and describe this true Church of Jesus Christ - which is the One, Holy, Catholic, Apostolic and Roman Church - we shall find nothing more noble, more sublime, or more divine than the expression 'the Mystical Body of Christ'" (section 13).

[21]Pope Paul VI, "Declaration on the Relation of the Church to Non-Christian Religions, *Nostra Aetate*," October 28, 1965, section 2, www .vatican.va/archive/hist_councils/ii_vatican_council/documents/vat-ii _decl_19651028_nostra-aetate_en.html.

[22]Pope Paul VI, "Dogmatic Constitution on the Church," chap. 4, section 33.

[23]Pope Paul VI, "Pastoral Constitution on the Church in the Modern World, *Gaudium et Spes*," December 7, 1965, preface, section 2, www .vatican.va/archive/hist_councils/ii_vatican_council/documents/vat-ii _const_19651207_gaudium-et-spes_en.html.

[24]Pope Paul VI, "Pastoral Constitution on the Church in the Modern World," part 1, chap. 2, section 28.

[25]Pope Paul VI, "Pastoral Constitution on the Church in the Modern World," part 1, chap. 4, section 43.

[26]"The Catholic Church," World Council of Churches, accessed October 11, 2019. https://www.oikoumene.org/en/church-families/the-catholic -church. See also, "Is the Roman Catholic Church a Member?," Frequently Asked Questions, World Council of Churches, accessed September 16, 2020, www.oikoumene.org/en/church-families/about-us/faq#is-the -roman-catholic-church-a-member-.

[27]Pope Paul VI, "*Evangelii Nuntiandi*," December 8, 1975, w2.vatican.va /content/paul-vi/en/apost_exhortations/documents/hf_p-vi_exh _19751208_evangelii-nuntiandi.html.

[28]"Ecumenical and Interreligious Affairs," United States Conference of Catholic Bishops Committees, accessed October 7, 2019, www.usccb .org/beliefs-and-teachings/ecumenical-and-interreligious/.

[29]Pontifical Council for Promoting Christian Unity, "Joint Declaration on the Doctrine of Justification by the Lutheran World Federation and the Catholic Church," October 31, 1990, www.vatican.va/roman_curia/pontifical _councils/chrstuni/documents/rc_pc_chrstuni_doc_31101999_cath -luth-joint-declaration_en.html.

[30]Three books by Lawrence Hull Stookey that outline the theology behind these changes are *Baptism: Christ's Act in the Church* (Nashville: Abingdon, 1982), *Eucharist: Christ's Feast with the Church* (Nashville: Abingdon, 1993), and *Calendar: Christ's Time for the Church* (Nashville: Abingdon, 1996).

[31]One history of this development is Thomas Bergler, *The Juvenilization of American Christianity* (Grand Rapids, MI: Eerdmans, 2012).

[32]Jason Byassee, "A Church of the Ages? An Ancient Incense," *Christian History* 129 (2019): 46-47.

[33]Pope Paul VI, "Address of Pope Paul VI During the Last General Meeting of the Second Vatican Council," December 7, 1965, w2.vatican.va/content /paul-vi/en/speeches/1965/documents/hf_p-vi_spe_19651207_epilogo -concilio.html.

Conclusion

[1]G. K. Chesterton, *Orthodoxy* (London: John Lane, 1909), 85.

[2]Chesterton, *Orthodoxy*, 194-95.

GENERAL INDEX

SCRIPTURE INDEX

INTRODUCTIONS IN SEVEN SENTENCES

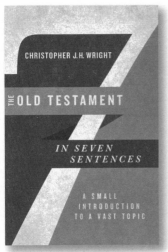

*The Old Testament in
Seven Sentences*
978-0-8308-5225-3

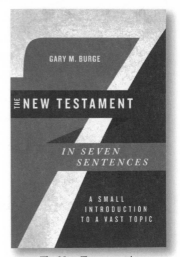

*The New Testament in
Seven Sentences*
978-0-8308-5476-9

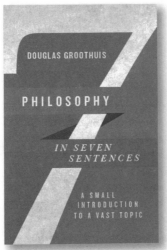

Philosophy in Seven Sentences
978-0-8308-4093-9